Achieve Your Own Emotional Branding

The Biology of Appealing to Emotions

Burc Uygurmen

Edited by Ken Stewart
Context Editorial Services

Cover design by BookTwoThree, NC

Table of Contents

Part 1

Part 2

Why I Wrote This Book

Actually, it was five years ago that I decided to write a book of my own.

Looking back now, I must admit that I had not had a real beating from life. Up to that point everything had gone smoothly.

I was good at my job, patient and passionate. I was well-intentioned and hard-working, but life had never really shaken me and dragged me down. In other words, I never had the chance to grow up. Who knows why, but in my mind I always had that scene of Bruce Willis in the movie Last Man Standing saying, "*No exceptions. Everybody pays the price...*"

Now I can see that it cost me a lot to gain the insight to be able to write this book. I lost a job that I really loved. This was followed by many rejections, which felt like falling from the top of a building with no parachute. I had to hide my broken self. I had to struggle for many months to be able get on my feet again, but still I couldn't avoid a divorce. In other words, life has since given me many chances to make a back payment for all the stairs that I had climbed so effortlessly.

As you read through these chapters, I hope you too gain insights into yourself that will make a profound difference in your life.

Here you will find how to create a more successful and fulfilled self-image despite the ambiguity and defeat you might face. Each section consists of examples, stories, proven theses and research that will help uncover the psychological and biological influences in your lives.

We can guarantee a more prosperous future by learning more and more about ourselves and eliminating the blind spots in our lives.

I can see myself waking up to a whole new life as my understanding of myself grows deeper each and every day. I hope that by the time you have finished the book, you too will be waking up to a whole new life.

1

How Does Our Brain Work?

Achieving your own Emotional Branding, the art of forming a relationship with others by connecting with their emotions, is an effective tool to strengthen your personal network and succeed in your endeavors.

In his book, *The Soul of Man under Socialism* (1891), Oscar Wilde says, "The emotions of man are stirred more quickly than man's intelligence" As an example, he points out that it is much more easy to have sympathy with suffering than it is to have sympathy with thought.

Emotions are the primary motivators of our behavior and they are contagious. The brain has many complex methods for detecting emotions in other people, and it uses this information to mirror their emotional state. That's the reason why we instinctively start distrusting someone when we feel we are not being trusted.

As our adult lives don't give letter grades, the reward of our life can only be measured by finding and walking a path that's good for us. In this walk of life, our decisions, thoughts and behaviors shape who we are and how we are being perceived.

The emotional value that we create and our ability to come off as likeable shape how we are sized up and treated by our peers.

Likable people are more likely to get help, be hired, get useful information from others and have mistakes forgiven. A study of 133 managers by researchers at the University of Massachusetts found that if an auditor is likable and gives a well-organized argument, managers tend to comply with his suggestions, even if they disagree and the auditor lacks supporting evidence.

Our feelings play a crucial role in influencing our decisions and thoughts. In our daily lives, we can observe that our emotional side and logical side are in constant conflict, and the winner is usually our emotions. For instance, our logical side tells us to lose weight, but succumbing to our emotions, we can eat a full bag of chips in one go.

Before we get into the subject of appealing to emotions and achieving your own emotional branding, let's have a look at how the brain works, because these thinking processes have great impact on your behaviors and preferences.

Chemical Cocktails in the Brain

Trust is an emotion highly related with love and submission.

According to the Plutchik's wheel of emotions, two most powerful primary emotions *joy* and *fear* form up their resulting emotions *love* and *submission* when they are combined with trust respectively. It also is one of the most important ingredients in any modern relationship.

But have you ever thought how we decide to trust someone? And does appealing to emotions have anything to do with trust?

In 2004, Neuroeconomist Paul Zak and economist Ernst Fehr have designed an experiment with a research team from Zurich University. They put 200 men on oxytocin or placebo and asked them whether they would split a $10 stake with a stranger. If the stranger accepted the offer, they were both paid, but if the offer was rejected, they both got nothing.

This game is designed to measure generosity and trust—defined as offering someone more than he or she needs. The study recently showed that those who inhaled a dose of oxytocin made offers that were 80 percent higher than those given a placebo. Moreover, subjects who received oxytocin did not demand more money than was offered.

These results suggest that oxytocin primes us to trust others by amplifying our empathy for others and motivating a desire to help them.[1]

Oxytocin is a simple molecule found only in mammals to make mothers care for their offspring. In humans, it is known to facilitate birth and breastfeeding in women. It increases connection, reduces anxiety and the fear of social betrayal[2] like the mother who is mentally ready for a child after six weeks of her pregnancy, while the father can't share the same feelings before he holds the baby and socialize with her.

---

[1] *"The Neurobiology of Trust*; Paul J. Zak; SCIENTIFIC AMERICAN, INC.; 2008

[2] "Oxytocin shapes the neural circuitry of trust and trust adaptation in humans"; Baumgartner T, Heinrichs M, Vonlanthen A, Fischbacher U, Fehr E; *Neuron; 2008*

Besides carrying the baby, the mother is engaged in a constant social interaction by sharing her feelings, food and oxygen with her throughout her pregnancy. This strong social interaction with the baby helps the mother release oxytocin which is also called the "love hormone."

One of the studies that was published in 2012[3] examined oxytocin levels in new lovers versus those in single people. It found that there were high levels of oxytocin in the first stages of romantic attachment, and these were sustained for six months by the high level of social interaction.

Did you ever think why we have a "love-relationship" with our vehicle, pet or our house?

That's also because we get socialized with them and through them. Our body releases oxytocin as a result of this social process and supports us to establish emotional bonds with our car, pet or partner.

As in this relation between oxytocin and trust, our behavior and feelings are powerfully affected by the biological cocktails in our brain and the meaning of events to the unconscious mind. Once we develop awareness around these processes and how they are impacting our lives, this will help us focus on changing our behaviors in order to achieve our own Emotional Branding.

---

[3] "*Oxytocin during the initial stages of romantic attachment: Relations to couples' interactive reciprocity*"; Schneiderman I, Zagoory-Sharon O, Leckman JF, Feldmana R, Psychoneuroendocrinology; 2012

Interpreting the New Information

As a trainer and a speaker, I offer business people corporate training sessions in the concept of Appealing to Emotions and Buying Habits.

I like to use music as a tool to create intimacy during the training, and when I start my classes with musical instruments around, I prefer to further draw people's attention with a single question: "Do you have any ideas about what kind of training we will experience today?"

I mainly get a few weak responses. One person asks, "Will you play guitar?" Another says, "Will you ask us to play?" or "I guess we'll have an entertaining day today!"

I reply by asking another question: "Have you ever observed frogs?"

After a few yes and no responses, I begin to explain.

Marketing guru Seth Godin says that people also behave like frogs in a certain way. Frogs have a way of waiting calmly to catch their prey. As soon as a frog sees a potential meal—a fly, for example— it jumps up and catches it with a flick of its tongue and then settles back down.

Like frogs, we also track the information that buzzes around us. As soon as we spot a unique bit of info, we grab it. Then we take a step back and predict the rest of the story based on our previous experiences.

For example, when we ask for directions, we usually don't listen to the answer to the end. As soon as we get that first bit of information, we prefer to predict the rest of the description according to our own knowledge.

Thus, how we say things and what we say first makes a huge difference in how we are interpreted or perceived.

I very well remember such a conversation in a family dinner.

When I decided not to continue my professional career but instead to start my own training firm, I told my family that I shall use music in my training sessions. Their first reaction was one of great sadness. Right away they asked, "How will you use music in your training?"

I watched their face grow more unhappy as I spoke. I remember how they asked, "Do you think you can earn well in music? Did you study and work all this time in order to be a musician?"

Had I really told them that I would be a musician or giving music lessons?

I had not, but my family's first reaction was to grab hold of the new information from my words. They instantly caught the words "music" and "guitar" and carried them to the category in their mind where other musical topics are stored; then "filled in" the rest of my story using their previous experiences. As a result, they totally misinterpreted my words. Unlike the image I was trying to paint, they had a picture of me giving music lessons and being a musician after all.

And what's worse, once our brain categorizes information, it immediately starts to weave a neural network around this new information and to create visualizations related to the new information. Once that process starts, it can be difficult to reverse. You can't put toothpaste back in the tube once it's been squeezed out.

In other words, once something you have said gets categorized within the listener's brain, it's almost impossible for external influences to remove it from that category and place it within another category. The only thing that can relocate the information is the listener's conscious will that will be influenced by new experiences or a very influential third-party.

Now, ask yourself these questions about your own habits: In the stress and hustle of modern life, can you take the time to deeply inquire into every piece of information you receive? Don't you generally focus on the negative and create your own worst case scenarios? Or do you usually simply interpret new information in light of your past experiences and knowledge? Isn't this selective perception the way our minds habitually categorize information?

Categorization

Daily life rushes by. It feels like 24 hours is not enough time in a day to finish our duties, maintain our relationships and build new ones; find spare time for ourselves and our family. With our increasing responsibilities, our time constraints are getting tighter and our brain needs to create shortcuts and "folders" more than ever. In the fast pace of life, our brain craves shortcuts that will ease our thinking processes, relax our mind and eventually save us time by categorizing similar information together in mental folders.

During the day we find ourselves under an intense bombardment of information. Besides endless phone calls, e-mails, social media messages and meetings, we are also being exposed to a great deal of information pollution.

Mark J. Pearrow, of the Massachusetts Institute of Technology, defines this information pollution as "Infobesity"[4]. Pearrow claims that we become addicted to the flow of information because it also triggers the reward mechanism in our brain the way sex, food, music and other elements of pleasure do.

Recall yourself scrolling down your social media news feed page. Sometimes it gets so appealing to go further down that we can't find the motivation to close the feeds page and get back to our daily life. We almost feel addicted to it for a time.

Under the bombardment of information, we can't even ask how and where to use the info that we receive during the day. This overwhelming flow of information changes our habits of saving and using the information gathered.

We tend to listen to and store the bits of information that align with our thoughts and ignore the ones that do not. This behavior is actually a reaction of our brain to protect our well-being. By ignoring the dissonant information, our brain tries to relax us rather than increase our stress level, which is already high due to our daily activities.

We must appreciate our brain's defense mechanism that's designed to protect our well-being whenever necessary.

---

4 "Infobesity: Cognitive and Physical Impacts of Information Overconsumption"; Mark J. Pearrow, Massachusetts Institute of Technology (2012)

Our brain reacts to horrifying memories and to diets in much the same way. Any kind of eating disorder, including diets, causes our brain to think that our body is in danger.

Just consider the eating habits of the first humans, who could eat only when they could access food but managed to maintain their weight level even if they went hungry for days.

Likewise, our brain again reacts to protect our well-being by causing us to regain weight whenever possible. Neuroscientist Sandra Aamodt says, "Several long-term studies have shown that girls who diet in their early teenage years are three times more likely to become overweight five years later." In five years, most people who go on a diet regain the weight they lost, and 40% of them gain back even more.

How Does Our Brain Categorize?

Our brain categorizes information rather like groceries are categorized in supermarkets. For example, supermarkets have a dairy products section and a low-fat milks section within that. This makes it much easier for us to find and compare the products we are looking for. To ease our thinking processes, our brain categorizes information by the same principle, under main and sub-categories.

For example, when we think of a dog, first our brain goes to that category of living creatures, then the category of animals and lastly activates the category that holds the visuals of the dogs we have seen before.

When you think of a hammer, this time your brain goes to the category of inanimate objects, then repair tools, and lastly the brain activates the category which has the visuals of the hammers that you have seen before.

However, the research[5] of Harvard University's Alfonzo Caramazza and his team shows that when people who are born non-sighted think of a certain object, the category area that is related with that object is also being activated.

Caramazza says that our brain does not only categorize by visuals, but is an organizational structure that stores related information together.

Let's think of some human names. Wouldn't you say that thinking of certain names recalls joy and trust but others recall insecurity and repulsiveness? That's because, when we think of a certain name, our brain goes to that category and recalls the common characteristics of the people we know by that name. Eventually the result is a shortcut and a prejudiced opinion.

---

5 "Category-specific organization in the human brain does not require visual experience"; Mahon, B. Z., Anzellotti, S., Schwarzbach, J., Zampini, M., & Caramazza, A.; Cognitive Neuropsychology Laboratory, Harvard University (2009)

For example, when you think of the name Sue, first your mind goes to that category and finds the visuals of the people you know by that name. Later, you recall the common attributes of those people.

If you think the common attributes of all the Sues you know are kindness and sensitivity, then this means that the name Sue is categorized in your mind by these attributes.

If you think of the name Alex and recall mainly egocentric and opportunist attributes, then this means that in your mind the name Alex is categorized with these attributes. When you meet with someone new named Alex, first you will have that prejudiced opinion about him because of your categorization.

Now let's check the attributes of certain names with someone near you. For example, when you ask one of your friends her opinion of people named Sue, she most probably would identify different attributes than yours, according to her own experiences.

Similar information can be categorized differently by different people, depending on their hereditary codes and life experiences. This means that we first have to understand the thoughts, experiences, expectations and priorities of the other party, preferably in the early stages of our relationship.

The best way to do this is by starting with a dialogue and asking questions to find out similarities and discover mutual experiences. Unfortunately in the fast pace of life we most of the time skip the dialogue part in our communications. But we should remember that by doing so, we also skip the chance to build an effective basis for our relationship.

Now let's talk about how we can use the categorization tool to start our communication one step ahead.

Like certain names recall certain attributes and the result is a shortcut and a prejudiced opinion, we should aim to be included in the appropriate categories in the other person's brain to utilize the shortcuts and prejudiced opinions that may serve us in the best way.

It would be wise to position ourselves with the information that fits our goals best. Focusing on similarities and similar experiences rather than differences helps to integrate us directly with these shortcuts and categories in the other party's mind.

And while integrating to these shortcuts it would be wise to use some *magic words*[6] that would touch some strings and directly reach their minds.

Mark Hayes says, "One of the most powerful words to use in your speech is *'You'*. It's more influential than words like *'money'* and *'sex.'* Whether we like to admit it or not, we're all a bit egocentric. We all want to feel that the conversation is all about us and there is no word in the language that can better do the job than any other word creating a powerful subconscious connection."

Another word that arouses our attention is *'New'*. When we see the word *'new'*, we subconsciously think improved and exciting. According to several behavioral psychology studies, new products, novel solutions, and a sense of adventure draw shoppers to products with the 'new' label. We have a positive

---

[3] *Magic Words That Increase Sales*, Mark Hayes (2013)

association with everything new - we're constantly wanting a newer car, new clothes, and the newest technology.

And the word **'Free'** isn't just a price - it's a powerful emotional trigger and a source of irrational excitement. You know that feeling when you get at a buffet, where you're full but you keep eating because it's free?

Gregory Ciotti, founder of Sparring Mind, argues that the word *'free'* exposes humanity's general aversion to loss. In economics, loss aversion describes the idea that people will frequently choose not to lose something (money) rather than to gain something, even something of relatively greater value.

The main idea of integrating to certain categories is to be able to first get into the *consideration set* of people who possess certain characteristics and personality traits. One way of doing this is by having a strong story that supports your characteristics and the other way is to display certain social behaviors.

If your lover values care and trust, remember that it would take more than words to be included in this category. Listening to her without interrupting and trying to understand her ambitions can be some of the behaviors that would help you to be included in the "care and trust" category in her mind. It is important to note that people are remembered by their behaviors rather than their words and the most effective and catchy way to communicate is by displaying certain social behaviors and characteristics.

For example, with someone who wants peace in her life, you might use many words to associate yourself with "peace" in her brain. However, if despite your words you once display repressive or aggressive behaviors, then you won't just be inconsistent; you will immediately be categorized in the "dissonant" category. The words you have used or any similarities you have discovered up to then would lose all their importance. Words will be forgotten but behaviors will remain.

In fact, *people do not care about what you say; they only care about how you make them feel*. That's the reason our words don't have the same permanent impact as our behaviors. We understand what's been said, but we remember how we were treated and how we felt.

We actually go to a concert because of the feelings that we are going to have by being there. The song lyrics only matter insofar as they have meaning for us, no matter how impressive they may be. We can say the same thing about a public speaker. We are more interested in listening to a role model who can influence us rather than the phrasemongering that we are going to get.

Now, before your next conversation, ask yourself: do you think your excitement should be only about the things you are going to say? Or should it be more about the value you are going to add by being a role model, able to influence the person you're speaking with?

Let me give an example from a panel that I participated in as a speaker. Like all of the speakers, the gentleman before me was supposed to give a 20-minute speech. Unfortunately he exceeded his time and stole five minutes from mine while ignoring the warning of the moderator.

Until then, he was actually giving a powerful speech about communication and expectations, but his indifference to his time constraint placed him right into the non-compliance category that he will always be remembered by.

His extra five minutes of speaking added nothing to the subject but he managed to get categorized as an oblivious person due to his behavior.

Aoccdrnig to a rscheearch at Cmabrigde Uinervtisy, it deosn't mttaer in waht oredr the ltteers in a wrod are, the olny iprmoetnt tihng is taht the frist and lsat ltteer be at the rghit pclae. The rset can be a toatl mses and you can sitll raed it wouthit a porbelm. Tihs is bcuseae the huamn mnid deos not raed ervey lteter by istlef, but the wrod as a wlohe.

We also read people that way: not word by word but as a whole.

2

Appealing to Emotions

According to the Meaningful Brands Survey which spoke to 50,000 consumers in 14 countries all around the world, 70% of the brands currently being used could disappear entirely and consumers wouldn't even realize it. That's a lot of brands, considering that an average household meets its basic supermarket needs with approximately 185 items.

Now let's consider the people you are connected to in your daily life or through social media, but this time instead of 70%, let's make them *all* disappear at once.

How would your life change if all the people you are connected to disappeared at once?

With most of them, you may hardly notice. For others, you would feel sorry but get over it in a short time, but a small number would be deeply missed.

In this section we will discover how those people who would be missed deeply were able to establish such deep and meaningful connections. We'll do this by comparing them to brands that appeal to emotions to create loyal customers.

Have you ever given a thought to why we go to shopping malls?

Well yes, shopping is an obvious reason, but in most cases we go to a mall without any need for shopping. We sometimes just go there to spend time, and we leave without buying anything.

You can hear your friends say, "Let's see the new mall that opened last week."

Let's think about this for a moment. Do they have anything to buy from that new mall? Or does this new mall have some brands that no other mall has?

Unlikely; your friends probably don't even know what brands have stores there.

We actually like to go to malls for social status. If the context of the mall suits our social status, we feel secure and a part of it. We proudly check in with our mobile devices, spend time with friends and enjoy a break.

The brands that we are loyal to and the people we are deeply connected with both provide the same social status, security and sense of belonging. Both are extensions of our self-image, which needs to be approved occasionally.

Brands and people have a way of representing certain qualities like leadership, passion, happiness, entertainment or convenience. Brands achieve this by marketing campaigns and slogans; people show these values by displaying certain characteristics through their behaviors.

For example, I may very much like to spend time with a friend who adds value to my life by inspiring me with his passion. Similarly, I may very much like to wear the products of a brand that uses visuals of passionate people in its marketing campaigns and uses "Impossible Is Nothing" as a slogan. Both experiences offer me the values of passion and feelings of inspiration.

Creating an İllusion

A certain cola brand uses the pleasure of crowded tables, the customs of specific communities and its slogan about happiness in its marketing campaigns in order to be stored in the happiness category, along with similar information. The "happiness" categorization of the brand creates a sense of belonging and trust long before the purchase of its product. And at the moment the need arises, these feelings turn into buying behaviors.

The contention between this cola brand's customers and those of its rival has been going on for a long time. For loyal customers, preferring one brand to another is almost a matter of life and death. Most of them argue that the other brand tastes awful.

However, numerous taste tests can be found on the Internet which show blindfolded subjects trying to guess which product belongs to which brand. The results are interesting. Most of the subjects who find the other brand's taste to be almost disgusting cannot distinguish between the products when they taste them while blindfolded. Literally, these tests show us the strong impact emotional branding has on our feelings and behaviors. Emotional branding can create an illusion about a product or a person by affecting the observer's feelings.

In his book[7], Rolf Dobelli mentions what he calls the "swimmer's body illusion." Our impression is that swimmers have perfect bodies because they train extensively. Dobelli says that's an illusion. Rather, they are good swimmers because of their physiques.

Similarly, consider the people who graduate from top-performing schools. Are they successful because these schools really offer the best possible education? Or do the schools only recruit the best-performing students, students who have great potential to be successful anyway regardless of the school's influence?

Like in the cola example, the illusion of one brand tasting much better than its rival is because of its successful emotional branding, not really because of the product itself. The brand that can appeal to emotions actually creates an illusion in how the product's taste is perceived.

Likewise, the individuals who appeal to our emotions also distinguish themselves from the crowd and create a similar illusion that we cannot explain unless we are aware of emotional branding principles.

Think of a friend you feel comfortable and happy with. You would categorize this person alongside similar life experiences and information, just as you would do with a brand that promises you happiness.

For many years, emotional brands have used emotional connotations to appeal to our feelings, so that the brand gets stored in certain categories in our mind.

---

[3] *The Art of Thinking Clearly*, Rolf Dobelli (2011)

As individuals we can also strengthen our relationships if we better understand the categories of the person we are communicating with and are able to appeal to these categories.

Understanding Expectations and Priorities

It's a fact that we can improve our skills and competencies in the long run. But in the short term, our skills are stable and fixed.

In Figure 1 let's use the **circle "S"** to represent our **Skills**.

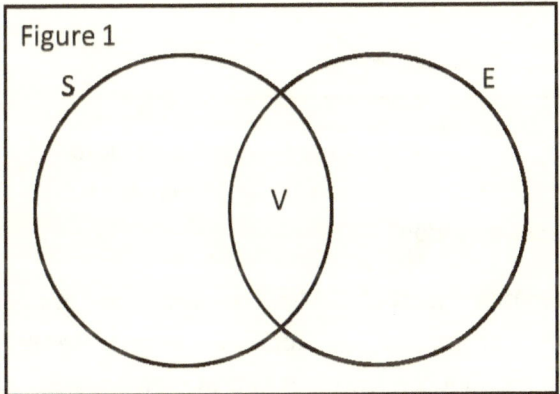

The people we relate to also have expectations and priorities from life and from others. Like our skills, these expectations are more or less stable in the short run. Let's use the **circle "E"** to represent the **Expectations** of the other people.

The **"V" circle**, the area where the two circles intersect, represents the **Value** that's been created by the correspondence of our skills with the other party's expectations. This means that the more we can match our skills with the needs and expectations of the other person, the more value we can create in this relationship. And because expectations and skills are both stable in the short run, the only way to expand the *value* area is by understanding the other person's expectations and using our skills to meet them. This is the only way we can achieve a wider "V" circle, like the one in Figure 2.

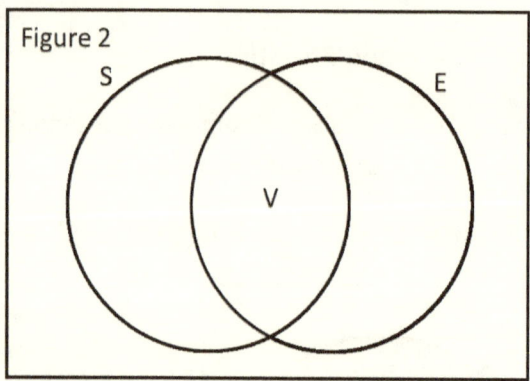

Figure 2

One Friday morning in January, world-famous violin virtuoso Joshua Bell played six Bach compositions over 45 minutes in a Washington, D.C. metro station[8].

During those 45 minutes, a total of 1097 people passed in front of him. Only seven of them stopped, even for a short while. Twenty people gave him money but continued walking at their normal pace. That morning Bell collected a total of $32. When he stopped playing, no one noticed or applauded and silence prevailed.

Nobody recognized him as one of the greatest violinists in the world, playing some of the most complex compositions ever written, on a violin worth $3.5 million. However, two days before this mini-concert, the tickets for his concert in Boston were sold out at an average price of $100 each.

---

[8] www.washingtonpost.com/wp-dyn/content/article/2007/04/04/AR2007040401721.html

This is a real story, a social experiment about perception and priorities that was conducted by the Washington Post.

Should we say that in this case Bell was incapable or untalented? Hardly. What this experiment shows is that our skills are not very useful when we don't use them according to people's priorities and expectations.

The intersection area in Figure 3 represents the value between Bell's skills and the commuters' expectations in this particular experiment.

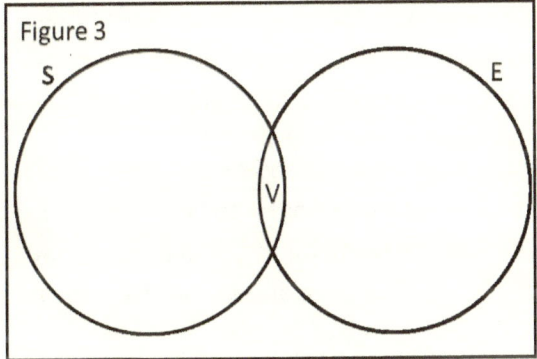

Figure 3

S   E

V

We expect exceptional service and a great atmosphere from a luxury restaurant. However, from a restaurant that we choose for a lunch break, we just expect quick service at a decent price.

If the restaurant we choose for lunch gives us great service along with a hefty bill, most probably we wouldn't make a second visit to that restaurant for lunch. This alone doesn't mean that it's a bad restaurant, but it surely means that the restaurant doesn't meet our expectations and priorities for a lunch break. We return late to work after paying three times the amount we'd normally pay. So the value we receive from that restaurant gets minimized.

Similarly, it's crucial for us to understand our communication partner's expectations and priorities in life and from particular occasions. Offering our skills and positioning ourselves with those priorities in mind will be beneficial to our relationship.

I remember a survey that asked numerous couples about their expectations from their relationships. Ask yourself the same question the survey asked:

What do you expect most from your partner in a relationship?

The survey found that the common phrase that everyone had agreed upon was, "I expect my partner to understand me." This result reminded me of George Orwell's famous quote, "Perhaps one did not want to be loved so much as to be understood."

Indeed, for our existence to make sense and for our lives to have meaning, one of the most important things is to be understood and hence to be valued. We may sometimes talk in a roundabout way, or our words may fall short or even offend, but deep down we really only wish to be understood.

And the best way to create an environment for open communication is first to understand ourselves and then others. Such understanding is vital in enabling us to appeal to another person's emotions.

To Create Max Value in Your Relations:

Do:
- ✓ Make a good observation of your communication partner's expectations and priorities from life and from you;
- ✓ Ask questions to understand and to start dialogues;
- ✓ Take the time to listen carefully and understand your communication partner.

Don't Do:
- ✓ Don't think everyone is going to give the same value to your skills and talents;
- ✓ Don't expect others to have the same life perspective as you do;
- ✓ If the context is not suitable, don't insist on starting the communication.

The Key to Happiness: Less Is More

How can we refute the assertion, "The more we own, the more freedom we have"?

This statement implies that:

We wake up freer when our quantity of clothes and shoes increases each and every day.

We are also free when we struggle to choose our 185 basic necessities from among those 40,000 products in the supermarket.

When our doctor offers us multiple options for treatment, we are also free to select the less risky one.

During the day, we generally have our laptop on one hand and our smart phone on the other, trying to deal with countless e-mails, phone calls and social media messages.

We seem free, but are we happy? In this world of free choices, are we able to really live in the moment?

Day after day we can watch ourselves turning into someone with more things but less happiness.

I call it *choice obesity*, this never-ending obligation to make choices along with the unhappiness that comes from increasing consumption. Considering the similarities in definition and results, don't you also think that it is as dangerous as obesity?

What initially comes to your mind when I say, "Less is more"?

We can briefly define this principle as achieving more by doing less, and in so doing, selecting the most important options and prioritizing them.

On one occasion I went to a restaurant in Munich that has a Michelin rating of two stars. The place is considered by many authorities to be one of the best places to eat in the city.

Along with a great atmosphere, the restaurant offered only four alternatives for each of the appetizer, main course and dessert sections in the menu. When I saw the menu, what came to my mind were some local luxury restaurants offering 50 different meals on their menus. I asked myself, "Do restaurants really need to offer 50 meals? Or is offering four of the best meals enough to make a restaurant stand out?"

Then I started thinking about myself and my relationships. Did I really need 50 people around me, most of them telling me how *not* to be able to achieve my goals? How much of my precious time was I spending to maintain those relationships? And were all these relationships ultimately helping me have a better life? Or were four people who make me happy and add value to my life just by their presence good enough?

I decided to reorganize my relationships even while I was contemplating the answers to my questions.

Like a gardener, I decided to prune the unnecessary time that I was spending on most people. Pruning actually lets plants grow by allowing the precious minerals to be used more effectively for the best results. So I have decided to prune my relationships to use my energy and time on the people who add value to my life.

I also started to question my position. In which category did I belong for other people? Did they feel comfortable and happy around me?

Was I acting like an individual who is consciously aware of his feelings and behaviors?

Was I open to criticism and feedback?

Was I well aware of my strengths and weaknesses?

Now, looking back on my life, I can easily see that the pace of modern life gives us no opportunity to achieve the necessary awareness to respond these questions accurately.

Our competition starts at the age of five. Kindergarten, elementary school, junior high, high school, university and college years pass swiftly, with so many hours of constant education and exams. Later our work life starts, with an even bigger workload and more stress. Then comes marriage and kids.

Suddenly we find ourselves at the age of 30-something and realize that we never had the time to observe and understand our real selves. Expectations and "the system" constantly push us to work and learn more. But we have to realize that constant learning and achieving self-awareness are totally different processes.

In this rushed, frantic pace, we actually never find time to question and think about the influences of our subconscious mind over our behaviors. Our mind is constantly preoccupied with questions of how to be and look more successful.

The more we focus on the obligations of life, the more we miss most of the realities of our actual self, which is strongly influenced by our subconscious mind. We find ourselves giving excellent advice to others that we've learned from the books we read, the quotes we see, or the training or seminars we attend. But it requires a greater effort to put our learning to work on our own automatic behaviors, which even we cannot fully acknowledge.

During this struggle of life, we also can't find any time to recognize our blind spots, which can only be observed by others and which have been governed mostly by our subconscious. We are running hither and thither trying to identify and categorize others without even knowing our actual selves.

Hey stop, we don't even know each other yet...

First we have to discover our psychological world, which is strongly influenced by our subconscious mind and which has great impact on our behaviors. Only then can we start working on our automatic behaviors in order to change our life.

Psychiatrist and Professor Nusret Kaya, who specializes in the psychophysiology of sleep, says that our unconscious mind, which plays a major role on our behaviors, begins to take shape in the womb.[9] As the stress of the mother increases, the baby will be born with a negative collective unconscious and without self-acceptance.

Doctor Kaya especially considers this to be very common in communities where there is inequality between man and woman and the female is under great stress. He claims that the conflicts and wars never end in such communities, where everyone is not treated as equals.

In order to have control over our subconscious behaviors, we first need to achieve significant self-awareness to be able to interpret the reasons behind our behaviors.

We will discuss these further in Chapters 3 and 5. Once we achieve this awareness, it works like a medicine to disarm our negative behaviors. And with some extra effort we can make a real difference in our behaviors, hence in our lives. We have to understand that this effort of changing our habits and the observation needed to achieve self-awareness do not happen overnight.

Dr. Phillippa Lally and colleagues from University College London recruited 96 people who were interested in forming a new habit such as eating a piece of fruit with lunch or doing a 15 minute run each day.[10] Participants were then asked daily how automatic their chosen behaviors felt. These questions included things like whether the behavior was 'hard not to do' and could be done 'without thinking'.

---

[9] Nusret Kaya; Evrensel Eşit Kuyruklu Canlı 2 (2011)

[10] *How are habits formed: Modelling habit formation in the real world*, Phillippa Lally (2009)

Although the average was 66 days, there was marked variation in how long habits took to form, anywhere from 18 days up to 254 days in the habits examined in this study. Drinking a daily glass of water became automatic very quickly but doing 50 sit-ups before breakfast required more dedication.

Achieving a change in our behaviors requires time. We can't heat up the room any faster by turning up the thermostat to the max level. It would heat up the room in the same amount of time whether you turn it up to the maximum degree or just to the desired degree. Likewise, we can't expect a change in our behaviors overnight. We need to be open hearted and open minded in this journey of recognizing our unconscious behaviors.

Many times in life we fail because we are oblivious to our subconscious behaviors. And because modern life constantly pushes us to enhance our skills and own more, we don't understand the reasons behind our failures.

But we need to understand that our success and happiness mainly depend on our behaviors rather than on our competencies or possessions. In its fast-flowing current, modern life does not give us any opportunity to develop any kind of awareness of these factors in our lives.

In this process of constant struggle, I saw the unintended discomfort that we cause to ourselves and to the people around us. I realized that behind our polished look we frequently cause disturbance to the people who are close to us. Much like the signboards that say *We apologize for the inconvenience* but that do not reduce the discomfort one bit.

If we resist criticism and feedback or ignore the influence of our subconscious mind on our behaviors, what we acquire from this book wouldn't go beyond memorizing words and sentences.

Now I can see myself changing into a more modest and happy man as my awareness grows. I feel like I am achieving more by following my dreams rather than the dreams of others or the expectations of society. And I see that I can only distinguish myself from the crowd doing what I am passionate about.

In her book *"The Top Five Regrets of the Dying"*[11] Bonnie Ware wrote about her patients who had gone home to die. She was with them for the last three to twelve weeks of their lives as a palliative care worker.

She wrote, "When questioned about any regrets they had or anything they would do differently, common themes surfaced again and again." Here are the five most common:

1. I wish I'd had the courage to live a life true to myself, not the life others expected of me.
2. I wish I didn't work so hard.
3. I wish I'd had the courage to express my feelings.
4. I wish I had stayed in touch with my friends.
5. I wish that I had let myself be happier.

At the end of one of her articles Ware emphasizes that we can all lead better lives by making wise choices. She says, "Life is a

---

[11] *The Top Five Regrets of the Dying,* Bronnie Ware (2012)

choice. It is YOUR life. Choose consciously, choose wisely, choose honestly. Choose happiness."[12]

Now, let's look at some statistics about our lives.

According to the Organization for Economic Cooperation and Development's *Better Life Index*, people in the United States work 1,787 hours a year, more than the OECD average of 1,776 hours. Around 11% of employees work very long hours, higher than the OECD average of 9%, with 16% of men working very long hours compared with 6% for women.[13]

According to the 2012 "Frozen Food Survey" of 1,256 people by the online research company DORinsight, one person out of three consumes frozen food at least once a week. Frozen food consumption increased by 10% compared to 10 years ago.

A study by TripAdvisor reveals that 50% of the people on vacation look at their business e-mails and call the office at least once while on vacation.

Most of us work harder than we used to work 10 years ago. We also arrive home later and more tired due to ever-increasing traffic.

We constantly bring work home because our mobile phone is always on and at arm's length; our personal life and business life are all entangled because of never-ending incoming e-mails.

We spend a large part of our day making decisions. As Herbert Simons revealed in the theory that brought him a Nobel Prize in

---

[12] www.inspirationandchai.com/Regrets-of-the-Dying.html

[13] www.oecdbetterlifeindex.org/countries/united-states/

the 1950s, our perfectionism and desire to be at our best all the time pulls us deeper into unhappiness and dissatisfaction. With each passing day our stress level increases, and the amount of time we spare for ourselves runs low.

Under this passive depression, our habits begin to change in order to relax our mind. Under constant stress, our brain thinks that our structure is in danger and needs to relax to protect our well-being. That's when our interest stirs for the brands and the people that appeal to our emotions.

Much like our constant desire for having an easy and fun shopping experience, we only want to be with others that we click with, who make us feel happy and who are well aware of their behaviors.

Think about the behaviors of the people who make you feel good. They are the ones who can act with empathy. We feel good and happy next to them regardless of their talents and wisdom. They are open to criticism and can make fun of themselves. They are not afraid to talk about their feelings.

And now ask yourself whether you are also displaying similar behaviors towards other people.

In this never-ending race to be successful and own more, do you recall any people who have parted ways with you because of your behaviors? Do you ever hide behind your blind excuse, "That's me, and I can never change"? Have you ever thought of your blind-spot behaviors that everyone can see except you? Would you like to try a different model—a model that suggests you might make yourself and others feel happier by owning less but behaving better?

To Be Happier:

Do:

✓ Instead of having a lot, have enough, so that you can spend more time enjoying what you have;

✓ Take a break to observe yourself and see how your emotions actually take control of your behaviors;

✓ Have your own dreams. Train yourself in order to achieve your dreams while you work for others who hire you to achieve theirs.

Don't Do:

✓ Don't be a perfectionist;

✓ Do not allow your personal life to become mixed up with your business life;

✓ Never ignore the effects of your fears and emotions on your behaviors.

3

What's Behind Our Behaviors?

Creating Value

What is value? And how can we explain it?

For example, when you want to buy a sweater because you feel cold, do you spend money because the sweater is woolly or because it will keep you warm?

In another words, do you actually spend your money on the product, or on the utility of the product?

Here, being made of wool is a sweater's *feature*, but the ability to keep us warm is the sweater's *value*. We actually never buy products but buy the value provided by the products. We buy the products' capability to satisfy our needs.

For our personal relationships, *we can define value as the sum of all the positive emotions and benefits we receive* from that particular person. We should also focus on the value that we create for others in a world where the value is more important than the product or the relationship itself.

Can you find a telephone that functions only as a phone today? We actually don't want a phone; we want the freedom to reach and to be reached at all times and everywhere. We want music not the CD, the movie not the DVD.[14]

Most of us have an electric drill at home. Do we really need the drill, which won't be used for more than five minutes in a year? Or do we just need the hole itself?

You may already be using some online brands like EBay, Amazon, U-Exchange or BarterQuest. Through these Internet sites, what is mine can be yours and vice versa with a few clicks.

The life cycle of tangible products has been extended enormously through online swapping and second-hand stores. Generally speaking, the demand for first-hand tangible goods is diminishing, but the demand to be able to access at all times, and be accessible at all times, increases.

The importance of appealing to emotions and emotional interactions will even continue to rise, as our urge to own things decreases and our needs shift from product to value.

Let's look at the most popular brands of our time like Google, Facebook, YouTube, and Twitter.

We use them many times during the day and there is no tangible product or service involved. These brands create perfect emotional values by promising us accessibility and providing us platforms to be unique story tellers.

As people get more stressed out, the emotional bond that we create and our similarities to others that we bring forward has recently become more important than our profession or which

---

[14]www.ted.com/talks/rachel_botsman_the_case_for_collaborative_consumption.html

brands we use. Trying to create such an emotional value requires energy and time but to give before we take would be a perfect start for a win-win based relationship.

By nature, as human beings we are more focused on the things that we can lose. For example when we start loving someone, we simultaneously feel the fear of losing that person and in most cases our fear weights our feeling of joy. You can see that there is a long list of locations where the lovers affix padlocks to fences, gates, bridges or similar public fixtures to symbolize their everlasting love and fear of loss.

So, why not create an emotional bond with others first to give them a gift that it will be hard to forsake?

Don't forget that successful people never negotiate over one topic. They always seek to increase options to be able to appeal to more than one interest or motivation. Two points form a line with a single opportunity but three points make an area where we can move in.

In our relationships we mainly position people by the value they create in our lives and by how they make us feel rather than by who they really are. No matter which benefits our relationship might depend on or how successful might that person be, we know that our relationship with someone with whom we don't feel good is not on solid ground.

For example, let me briefly tell the story of my two old friends who decided to be partners in order to start a law office.

At first glance, they seemed to be getting along well, but they were actually tolerating one another. In fact, most of their friends could see what they couldn't; that they actually possessed opposite personalities and there was almost no emotional value involved to maintain their relationship.

At first everything went smoothly. In time, however, they realized that maintaining a business relationship depends mostly on human relations rather than on knowledge and skills. As a result, they put an end to their partnership after about a year.

What was the real reason behind the failure of this lucrative business relationship?

Well, as in all partnerships, my friends started their business sharing a common purpose and mutual goals. But over time, their real characteristics and "subliminal-mind-controlled routine behaviors" started to show up.

Ultimately their long-term goals and points of view diverged distinctly. Common goals had been forgotten. Distinct, individual short-term and long-term goals loomed large. And with gradually deteriorating communication processes, they eventually began not sharing their individual goals with each other.

As a result, having no personal value to build a golden bridge between them, they became two individuals looking in completely opposite directions.

Our subconscious mind controls all of our automatic behaviors. And because of the unconscious behaviors it displays, our *alter ego* is believed to be our "second self" that is somehow distinct from our original personality. So all of our routine behaviors are being automatically ruled by subconscious principles and codes in order to relax our mind and ease its burden, since our mind is already under great stress.

Our mind actually possess more info and data than we need. Because it's impossible to process them all, our subconscious mind uses shortcuts that will ease our thinking processes. Our conscious mind actually provides 5% or less of our cognitive (conscious) activity, otherwise our heads can explode overwhelmed by the majority of data we have.

While driving, we sometimes notice ourselves driving to point A, when our original intention actually was to drive to point B. We pay attention to all the traffic signs and signals on the road, but where we're going is not where we first intended to go. In this case we realize that it was our subconscious mind that was driving the car until that moment. This is called *Automaticity* in social sciences.

Nowadays, firms are looking for individuals who accord with the company's mission and vision and who also have strong communication skills. Those qualities now mean even more than the person's professional aptitude. This shows that all work-efficiency processes mainly depend on individual personality and value rather than capabilities.

Whether it's our boss, colleague, customer or friend, everyone likes to maintain relations with other people with whom they click and feel comfortable. This individual *value* is even more important than the work itself, because at the end of the day it will determine the quality of the work being done.

Understanding the Shift

When John Cage first released his composition *4'33"* in 1952, everyone greeted his work with great surprise. The song consists of four minutes and 33 seconds of silence. After so many years, he can still make people talk with interest about him and his work.

Remember when free e-mail and social networking sites first emerged? We also greeted them with great surprise. Many years later we realize that investing in people and establishing a loyal customer base by creating value is more beneficial and lucrative than any subscription fee.

Now we are in a new era where consumer habits are changing enormously. The new generation is demanding to be listened to and to be valued more than any generation before them. The way we communicate and do business may totally change in a few years.

We used to make a first impression by our physical appearance, our dignity or the brands that we own.

Now, we mostly provide a first impression by our online profile. And our online impression does not only depend on our personal info; it also depends on the type of information that we share or that's been shared about us by others.

Our reputation is no longer measured only by our social status, the car we drive or the mobile phone we use; now it's measured by the status updates we share, the profile pictures we display or the places where we check in.

As individuals we have to consider our consistency and trustworthiness in social media and in Google searches. Our online profile now plays a major role in determining which doors will be opened for us, making it almost more important than our actual profile by the fact that it creates or axes the opportunity to move to the next level of communication.

Now it is possible to reach almost everyone and everything from Google. Online shopping has started to replace regular shopping habits. The success of a store is not measured only by its physical appearance but also by the online reviews and ratings it receives.

The same shift happens with one-on-one sales too. Here is how Bernard Marr who is a globally recognized expert in strategy, performance management and analytics puts it, "Imagine buying a car five years from now. The picture that comes to mind is the sales man in a suit that approaches you when you enter the car show room; he invites you to his desk, takes notes of your interests and then recommends a car you might want to consider. The sales rep would then take you through the different range, color and accessory options before handing you a brochure and giving you the option of arranging a test-drive at some point in the future"

"Based on extensive research and customer feedback, this traditional sales process is one that clients are currently getting rid of. Most customers that walk into a car showroom today will have done several hours of research online and usually know exactly what they want – often to the last detail. They come to the showroom to 'experience' the car, to sit in it, touch it, smell it and drive it." (Bernard Marr, Sales People: Do We No Longer Need Them?, 2014)

In this psychological jungle, appealing to emotions and creating personal value will come into value significantly. As with Cage's work, we don't need to like or appreciate these major changes in modern communication, but we surely have to understand them.

To Create Value in Your Relationships:

Do:

✓ Focus on how you make people feel, instead of on who you are and what you do;
✓ Take time to observe the conflicts that occur due to your automatic unconscious behaviors;
✓ Remember the reasons why you decided to get into a business or personal relationship with somebody. Watch your step; it can also be you who are causing the conflict.

Don't Do:

✓ Don't think that only others change. It can be you who has changed;
✓ Do not only measure the value you create by the material benefits that you provide;
✓ Don't let your emotions govern your behaviors.

The Influence of Emotions on Our Behaviors

Try to think of some occasions where our emotions take control of our behaviors.

For example, right before we make a public speech or take an important exam, no matter how much we have studied or prepared, our hands begin to sweat and our muscles start to get tense.

Think of your last five minutes before the exam starts. All the answers that were in your mind just an hour ago may feel like they have disappeared or been erased from your memory. Our emotions take control of our mind and body.

We try to avoid this emotional invasion and relax by trying to remind ourselves how prepared we were just an hour ago. But no matter how prepared or knowledgeable we are, our emotions can dominate our body the way a defense mechanism would.

The fiercest moments when our emotions take control of our behaviors may be when jealousy prevails. As the author of the novel we write in our head, we become so obsessed that we can turn into somebody else in a second.

Did you know that jealousy is the top reason for spousal murders in the U.S.?

Acting with our emotions can also make us do many painful things, like wearing high heels, having plastic surgery or getting a tattoo. If there were no emotional impact to them, why would we tolerate the suffering they inflict?

There is a huge marketing and advertising industry benefiting from the fact that our emotions have such a great influence on our behaviors.

For example, why did you make your last purchase?

You might say there was a good discount being offered.

And did you really need that particular piece?

Most probably not.

Take soda for example. Soda is soda, right? Does it really matter where it comes from or how it tastes? A soda brand from a well-known producer, with premium packaging and a fancy name, could be sold at three times the price of an average soda product. Moreover, we can see this particular brand not only in luxury restaurants but also in almost every supermarket, proving its demand.

Rather than the product's functionality, we make our purchasing decisions by our emotions. We first feel, then buy and then start to consider whether the product is suitable for us. Our subconscious brain functions with models, principles, values and rules. In fact, in most cases we don't even know what we are thinking.

In an experiment[15], a certain number of jams were tasted by students and experts. The result was that both groups gave the same ranking for taste. This means that one does not have to be an expert to choose jams.

Later the packaging of the same jams was changed and the jams were tasted by a different group of students. This time, when the packaging changed, the "likings" changed too. Although the jams were the same, the second ranking was completely different from the first due to the impact of the packaging.

And lastly, a third group of students tasted the jams. They were again asked to rank them, but this time with explanations of why

---

[15] *How We Decide,* Jonah Lehrer (2010)

they liked each jam better than the lower-ranked one. When thinking was involved, the rankings again changed completely.

The results of this experiment show that the choices we make with our emotions versus those we make with our rational mind may diverge from one another, even though the options are the same.

We may even come to a different conclusion when we think about why we like something. Maybe we should change all research methods that are based on asking direct questions about products or services, because the questions that lead us to think and answer don't reflect the real choices we make with our emotions and with the influence of our subliminal mind.

Have you ever heard of Pavlov's dogs?[16]

Every time the dogs were served food, the person who served the food would ring a bell. Therefore, the dogs reacted as if food was on its way whenever they heard a bell. Their saliva would begin to pour even when there was no food around.

Similarly, we are also being seduced by the impulse of pleasure that's been created long before we even see the product, and these messages of pleasure from our subconscious mind arouse us to purchase that specific product when the time comes that we need it.

Here, it would be useful to talk briefly about our personal and collective unconscious. Austrian neurologist and psychiatrist Sigmund Freud believed that the unconscious depends exclusively on the individual alone. He determined that our automatic

---

[16] "The Nobel Prize in Physiology or Medicine 1904". Nobelprize.org. Nobel Media AB 2013. Web. 19 Nov 2013. www.nobelprize.org/nobel_prizes/medicine/laureates/1904/

behaviors are shaped by our repressed and unexpressed emotions, perceptions, principles and individual experiences.[17]

In his psychoanalytic theory he claims that subconscious thoughts can surface and be embodied in symbolic forms in dreams, slips of the tongue and also by the content of our spontaneous jokes.[18]

Carl Jung, on the other hand, tells us about a distinct collective unconscious. He says the collective unconscious is inherited and cannot be explained by anything in the individual's own life. It consists of archetypes, pre-existent forms which can only become conscious secondarily.[19]

And Dr. Clotaire Rapaille positions himself between Jung and Freud by a third approach, the collective cultural unconscious.[20] His research majors on cultural codes. He determined that people define products, services and relationships by the cultural codes and characteristics that take place in their subconscious mind.

Let's take love for instance. Rapaille's research shows that different cultures have various identifications for love. French equate love with passion; Americans with needs and heartbreaks; Italians with pleasure and fun. On the other hand, Japanese identify love as a temporary decease.

[17] Westen, Drew (1999). "The Scientific Status of Unconscious Processes: Is Freud Really Dead?" Journal of the American Psychoanalytic Association 47 (4).

[18] Modell, Arnold H. "Psychoanalysis, Neuroscience and the Unconscious Self." Psychoanalytic review 99.4 (2012): 475-83.PsycINFO.

[19] *The Archetypes and the Collective Unconscious,* C. G. Jung (London 1996)

[20] "Marketing to the Reptilian Brain"; Dr. Clotaire Rapaille; Forbes 03 July 2006: 44. Business Source Premier. EBSCO. Web. 15 June 2010.

The brands that appeal both to our personal and collective unconscious simultaneously and consistently achieve a strong connection with our minds, though we cannot even put into words why.

For example, in the early 1990s an SUV brand conducted some surveys of its target audience to try to regain market share, but the company couldn't come up with a meaningful result. When Dr. Clotaire Rapaille analyzed the answers from the surveys, he realized that a common characteristic was regularly being repeated in the stories of the consumers. In their recollections many people mentioned open plains, the American West and riding free. From this perspective, the company judged that the code for this brand in the consumers' minds is a horse, which is a true representative of American Western culture.

All product updates and marketing campaigns were designed to support this image. The headlights became round just like the eyes of a horse. The new ad campaigns and visual changes worked well, and sales figures started to rise with the vehicle's new image.

In this example, what actually increased sales was not a newly added or updated functional feature. It was all about creating an emotional branding that appealed to the subconscious of the consumers' mind.

Now, let's try to analyze our daily life preferences by the same approach.

Why do you think you have only a few favorites from all the numerous cafés or restaurants in your town?

Because of the taste or the freshness of their products?

Or are the cost-free benefits and services they offer what makes those places different?

Your favorite restaurants' gardens, location, smell, generous portions or friendly waiters may be appealing to your emotions and subconscious mind. These all are actually the free-of-charge benefits of a restaurant. While you think it's the products that catch you, the reason you pick a restaurant might be due to the cost-free advantages of the place that touch some strings in your mind.

Most of the time, the social benefits in a workplace, like being understood or feeling valued, feels even more crucial than the salary we get.

Even before we go to another job interview, we first consider the cost-free social benefits of our job before any salary comparison. Most of the time, these social benefits are much harder to give up than any monetary benefits.

We could say much the same thing about the people we feel happy with, though we cannot put into words why we feel that way. People who appeal to our subconscious mind earn a distinguished place in our life. The people we relate to who use emotional branding tools successfully by appealing to the codes and perceptions in our mind manage to maintain distinguished relationships. We will study these steps in the next chapter.

More than two thousand years ago the Greek philosopher Aristotle determined that there are mainly three influences in persuasion[21]:

- **Ethos**: Reliability and Credibility
- **Pathos**: Emotional Interactions and Imagination
- **Logos**: Logical Interactions and Consistency

For example, Martin Luther King, Jr.'s *"I Have a Dream"* speech dated August 28th, 1963 is a very good example of Pathos, which mainly appeals to emotions.

---

[21] *Rhetoric*, Aristotle, 350 B.C.E

Ben Bernanke's *"The Economic Outlook and Monetary Policy"* speech dated August 27th, 2010 is a good example of Logos, which mainly addresses logical arguments.

Our logical and emotional brain are in constant conflict, and our emotions, is usually the winner. For example, when buying a car our logical side tells us to settle for the less-expensive model, but succumbing to our emotions, we might even go into debt to buy the one that attracts us.

Ultimately, rather than one side of our brain dominating the other, we need to be using both our logical and emotional brain simultaneously and consciously for successful communication and a controlled life.

For instance, women are more successful in using their emotional side in communication, while men are more successful at managing their own emotions. Looking back to our daily interactions, we can easily observe a woman being more persuasive by appealing to emotional inducements, yet succumbing to her intense emotions in emergency situations, while men tend to be more calm and solution-oriented in similar situations.

We have great potential to use both sides of our brain to build solid relationships and enrich ourselves by appealing to both emotions and logic. But before that, to achieve true control of our mind when needed, we need to observe and work hard on those actions that are stimulated by our emotions. We also need to acknowledge and master our logical mind in order to strike a balance when our emotions start to dominate our actions.

Having control over our emotions and emotion-based actions is obviously easier said than done, since these actions include subconscious interactions. We will discover practical techniques to be able to achieve emotional control in Chapter 5.

4

Achieving Your Own Emotional Branding

"East" and "West" are two of the first emotional brands that we learn. They evoke a deeper identity and meaning than "North" and "South."

At first glance they may only seem like simple definitions; however, they truly express a distinct value by the unique characteristics, culture, traditions and social status of the areas they refer to.

The first categorization of "East" and "West" in our minds takes place visually, on a map. Then we fill in the rest of their significance through the learning process.

Essentially, we feel ourselves closer to one side or the other. If we were to buy a product or a service, our emotional sympathy towards one side may influence us even more than the price or the quality.

Kevin Roberts, CEO of the Saatchi & Saatchi advertising agency, says that the most striking reason for appealing to emotions is the increasing rate of people becoming isolated and lonely.[22]

---

[22] *Lovemarks – The Future Beyond Brands,* Kevin Roberts, Saatchi & Saatchi Books, (2006)

In an interview in Capital magazine he said, "Today's consumers want to establish connections with the brands in many ways. They look out for new emotional links. There are many people living alone, and in ten years their number will increase even further. There are seven million people living alone in England. And this is three times what it was 40 years ago. In 2020, 40% of the households will consist of a person living alone."

Ironically, as the emotional links between people weaken, "Emotional Brands" come to the rescue to fill up the gaps.

Consumers prefer brands that establish emotional bonds. Those brands that appeal to emotions stand out from the crowd. Because they are preferred by more people, they also generate more income. Kevin Roberts emphasizes this by adding, "Money can't buy love, but love can make you earn more."

The rate of loneliness is increasing, and brands invest in different marketing methods to fill this gap. As individuals we also have an effective tool to strengthen our personal network and relationships: Achieving our own Emotional Branding.

We should never underestimate the important role of feelings in our decisions. People always seek out self-beneficiary situations, and one of the most effective and cost-free ways you can benefit someone's reward mechanism is through the feelings that you generate by your behaviors.

For example, when I am hiring someone or getting into a business relationship, I can't say I make my decisions just by looking at the hourly rate or portfolio of that person. Rather, I first decide based on my emotions towards him. If I feel that I can click with that person and communicate easily, then I also feel like the quality of the process will affect the quality of the outcome.

Eventually the quality of the outcome may or may not be better than those of other candidates, but ultimately the way I feel plays a stronger role while imagining the possible results of this relationship.

It's a fact that we all make our decisions based on our emotions. We may think the process of buying a product or an idea goes like this: Think ⟶ Buy ⟶ Feel.

However, the process actually works like this: Feel ⟶ Buy ⟶ Think.

We first *feel* for a product or an idea, then buy it, and then we try to bring logical explanations to our decisions. Again, our subconscious brain uses modeling, principles, values and rules. In fact, in most cases we don't even know what we are thinking.

Think about your most important decisions:

Your spouse, your job, your college degree...

Can you say that you made logical choices by rationally comparing all prospects while you were making the most important decisions of your life? Or did you basically rely on your emotions, as in many other life situations?

Appealing to emotions and acknowledging the secrets behind our behaviors are the revolutionary keys for a successful life.

We may not open every door by spending money, but making emotional investments in people may open many doors that look impossible for us.

Here is how.

Steps to Achieving Your Own Emotional Branding:

1. Visuality

Take a look at the image below and think of one or two things that come to your mind about that woman.

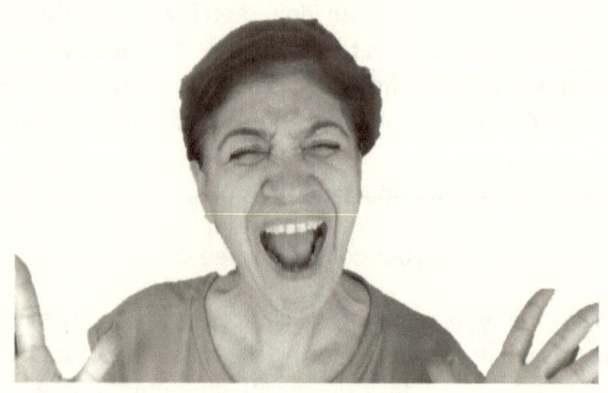

She looks angry and aggressive, right?

And how many seconds did it take to make your first comments?

Most likely, it took about three or four seconds to form your first opinions.

We form our initial opinions towards a visual with our "fast" thinking. Neurologists say that we decide whether to rely on someone or do business with them within the first three seconds of our meeting.

Now let's try something else: multiply 18 and 26 without using a calculator.

How long did it take?

If you tried to find the result, most probably your pupils got bigger, your muscles tensed and you spent much more time and energy than you did in forming your first opinions about the woman in the picture.

And even if you didn't try the multiplication problem, would you agree that it would probably take more than 15 or 20 seconds to find the result?

Situations that require us to think on a subject demand more time and energy than interpreting a visual does. So we might call it our "slow" thinking.

Briefly, our brain has two kinds of thinking processes: slow and fast[23]. When we see a person, a store, an image or an interior decoration, we make our first opinions by using our fast thinking. Later comes our slow thinking, where we start evaluating certain attributes and making analytical deductions.

And simply this time difference between fast and slow thinking determines our perceptions and reactions towards our daily interactions; it also makes the visuality a powerful tool for emotional branding.

When we enter a store, we make our first assessments by looking at its appearance. Later we start thinking about buying something or trusting the employees. If we didn't like the store's appearance, we would feel an urge to leave the store before we even think about the quality of the store's products or employees.

---

[23] *Thinking Fast and Slow*, Daniel Khaneman (2011). *Brain Tricks—This Is How Your Brain Works*, Mitchell Moffit and Gregory Brown

Our fast thinking influences our slow thinking, because it analyzes the images almost immediately. After all, the store's present appearance has nothing to do with product quality or the reliability of the employees, but because our fast thinking comes first, it plays a dominant role in all of our decisions.

The same thing applies when we meet someone new. We form our first impressions according to the person's appearance. Our impressions may be totally different from the actual background of this person. Still, our first visual interpretation defines how we categorize the person in the first place. Then we spend the rest of our time with this person searching for clues to justify our first opinions.

How many people do you communicate with on your way from home to work or school?

One? Two?

Would you believe me if I told you that you actually communicate with numbers of people on your way?

The reason is that communication is not only verbal. You acknowledge some of these people with a nod of the head because of your first impressions of them; you may turn your head away because you find some of them irritating; you may display a certain attitude or set the tone of your voice just from looking at their appearance.

Eventually, all these preferences constitute your nonverbal communication towards the people you encounter along the way. And since you don't have any previous history with those people, you form all of your communication preferences just by looking at their appearance.

Sometimes we also verbally communicate with people we've never met before, as when we ask for an address or exchange money. In such cases we may realize that the person we first evaluated by his appearance is actually tougher or more naïve than we first thought. But to be consistent, we generally prefer to maintain our first attitude or tone of voice even if it means behaving like someone else.

Research conducted at New York University revealed that people form an average of 11 opinions towards the other person in the first seven seconds of communicating.

We can further divide this time into two segments of three seconds plus four seconds. In the first three seconds we form our first impressions, using our fast thinking to analyze all of the visual cues we see—the "visuality." Later we try to expand and solidify our first opinions by observing the body language, tone of voice and word selection of the person.

When we meet someone new, we have a tendency to visually compare her with the people we know. Referring to her visual appearance, our brain scans the people we already know to find similarities and makes the first analysis by the visual resemblances. This happens in the first three seconds of our communication.

Sometimes we stare at someone and say, "Wow, what a resemblance; he looks just like Mike." The first area in our brain where we will categorize this person will be in the same place as Mike.

Or we say, "Look at how he dresses; he's a real hick." In the first three seconds, our brain makes the first categorization by matching this person with someone we know who also dresses like that. And in the next four seconds we complete our character analysis by observing his body language and behaviors.

Professor Alex Matkovsky, of The University of Moscow's Department of Psychology, states that 56% of our communication occurs with our body language, 39% with the tone of our voice and 5% with the words we use.

Try to visualize the body language and posture of the most successful people you know. More than the words they use, we mostly remember their nonverbal communication—the tone of their voice or how they use their body. They stand tall, shake hands firmly, smile and look you in the eye when they speak to you. They pay attention to their shoes, hair and appearance, and their energy is always high. The way they dress and behave appeals to our fast thinking and creates an illusion.

With their firm smile, confident handshake, straight posture and high energy, effective people attract others by sending out positive signals. These positive signals affect their audience's energy and create a feel-good factor.

We can't deny that physical attractiveness is a strong psychological influence. In 1990, a study of 74 defendants conducted in Pennsylvania courts yielded some unexpected results. The defendants who were more handsome than others received significantly less punishment, even though the cases were similar.[24]

In a staged negligence trial, researchers looked at the part physical attractiveness played in the amount of damages that

---

[24] Castellow, Wuensch and Moore, (1991); Downs and Lyons (1990)

were awarded. When the defendant was more handsome than his victim, the defendant only had to pay an average of $5,600 in compensation. On the other hand, when the victim was the more attractive man, the average compensation was around $10,000.[25]

Since our childhood, all the heroes in movies were selected from personable people. Similarly, people who became role models to us throughout our lives were all impressive people. For this reason, being good looking and impressive, and being good or successful, are usually categorized in the same place in our minds.

Due to our visual fast thinking, in similar cases our brain goes to the category of handsome people and finds the related good qualities of the people who are categorized in the same area. Eventually visuality prevails and affects our decision in favor of the good looking.

---

[25] Kulka and Kessler (1978)

To Be Able to Use Visuality Well:

Do:
- ✓ Look confident by standing tall; look positive by smiling; look enterprising by being energetic;
- ✓ While talking, look people in the eye to show them that you are listening and that you care;
- ✓ Pay attention to your hair, your shoes and how you dress.

Don't Do:
- ✓ Don't dress like a character that you wouldn't like to reflect;
- ✓ Don't dress inappropriately for the place you are visiting;
- ✓ Adjust your appearance and posture but do not imitate.

2. Using Questions

Whether it's with someone you've already known or have just met, the best way to begin a communication process is by starting a dialogue, and the easiest way to start a dialogue is to ask questions.

Whether you are doing sales, leadership, marketing, recruiting someone or firing someone—whatever you are doing—always start with dialogue. Caring for people, giving value and highlighting our similarities are the fundamentals of our lives.

We can talk to people with an intention to start a dialogue, but can we be sure that the other party actually listens to us or is at least ready to listen to us?

Questions trigger the listener's brain to start working and focus on the subject. And most importantly, questions give us an opportunity to catch similarities. By listening carefully to the answers and by highlighting similarities, we can create a great starting point for ourselves to begin appealing to emotions and show the other person that we care.

Don't forget, people tend to listen to the information that relates to them, can benefit them and harmonizes with their thoughts; and they tend to ignore information that's the opposite. For example, if I support the Republican Party, I would tend to ignore all your positive comments about the Democratic Party and unconsciously turn a deaf ear to them.

Seth Godin says, "People don't believe what you tell them. They rarely believe what you show them. They often believe what their friends tell them. They always believe what they tell themselves." (Seth Godin, Q&A: Tribes and The Reality of Worldview, 2013)

The only way we can influence someone to give us the answer we desire is by asking him the right questions, the questions that will lead him to that result. The side that asks the questions actually leads the dialogue. Think for a second: who in your life is proficient at using questions?

Women and children are very good at leading discussion by asking questions.

For example, from another room I once unintentionally overheard my friends' conversation about a high credit card balance. When my friend asked his wife about her high credit card debt, she first reacted with a question like, "Really, why?" By asking an innocent question, she immediately softened the situation.

Then he said, "I don't know; let's take a look at your spending," and she immediately asked a second question to buy time, like, "Are you accusing me of overspending?"

He said, "It's your credit card we're talking about." She replied, "Don't you remember the present we bought for your mom? And how many times did you see me making a big purchase?" And the questions went on and on and on.

Ultimately it became my friend's fault for bringing up the subject.

While talking with someone who is angry or in a negative frame of mind, asking questions will give you many opportunities to take his mind away from those negative thoughts and use emotional and logical interactions to lead him to a desired state of mind.

We mainly ask questions to gain information or to give messages. We use information-gathering questions to be able to learn more, discover similarities and reveal cultural codes in the other person's subconscious mind. And even though we know the answer, we use message-giving questions to "adjust the frequency" of the conversation and to lead the other party to the desired answer.

For example, when we say to someone, "You would maintain a relationship with someone because it makes you feel good, right?" we mainly do it to lead the person to our frequency.

There are three main types of questions:

Closed-ended questions are the ones with a "yes" or "no" answer. If you ask them at the beginning of the conversation, they establish a strong basis to draw the subject to the desired place because of the influence of *consistency*, which we'll discuss in a moment. They are not good for information gathering, because the answers to these questions are plain and simple. For example: "Would you like to eat something?"

Open-ended questions like "what?" or "how?" are questions that require the responder to explain. They are great for discovering similarities and learning more about our communication partner. For example: "What kind of food do you like to eat?"

Leading questions lead the other party to give the answer you would like to get. These are generally used to give messages and are widely used in company meetings or presentations. There are mainly three types of leading questions:

- **Questions ending with "right?":** We first specify our opinion and then lead the person to that idea. For example: "We'll eat together, right?"
- **Dichotomous questions:** They mainly lead the other party to select between two alternatives. For example: "Would you like to have vegetarian or meat?"
- **Expert-opinion questions** first state the opinion of someone who's considered an expert in the subject at hand, or they may present some research finding that is already accepted by a vast number of people. Next comes an open-ended question. For example: "Experts suggest we should eat often but in smaller portions. It's been three hours; I think we'd better get a menu. What would you like to eat?"

Use leading questions only when you want to reach specific conclusions and achieve specific results. Using leading questions constantly will damage the quality of your conversations and will categorize you as a manipulative person.

Ultimately, we should choose our questions according to the conclusions we want to reach. Every question has to have a purpose. Aimless questions waste time and create conflict without making any real contribution to the dialogue.

Observe the purposes of the questions around you. Are they mainly about the past and about what has happened? Or are they about the future and solution-oriented?

Asking the right questions will carry you to the results and solutions you want, but asking the wrong questions breeds deadlocks and vicious cycles.

Have you ever traded funds or stocks? Or placed bets?

Let's say you have a tip from one of your friends after you made a bet or bought stocks; would you change your bet or sell your stocks?

Often people making bets and trading funds believe that their first choice is always right.

Why could that be?

Because once we make a choice and stand up for an idea, we prefer to resist all pressure to change our mind in order to behave and look *consistent*,[26] even though we know that we are not right in our decision, and even though the source of this pressure is our own mind.

Have you ever watched the televised singing competition *"The Voice"*? On this program, four judges are seated with their backs to a contestant. When the contestant begins to sing, the first judge to press a button gets to be that singer's coach for as long as they remain in competition.

---

[26] *Influence: The Psychology of Persuasion, Consistency*, Robert Cialdini (1984)

Once a judge presses the button to select a singer and turns around to him or her, we notice that the judge who made her selection laughs and applauds—even if the singer's performance starts to go bad and she starts hitting the wrong notes.

That's actually a funny moment, because all the other judges who didn't turn around can be seen grimacing at the sour notes. But the first judge has already made her selection. Do you think she's going to show herself to be inconsistent by opposing her own decision in front of millions of viewers?

In such cases, *people strive hard to be consistent with their first choices because consistency evokes mental strength.*

We can see this in romantic relationships, too. Once we commit to a love relationship, we tend to validate this person to ourselves and to our acquaintances, insisting that she is the right person for us. In this way, we resist all contrary insights or opinions. For the sake of proving our consistency, we often ignore our own unhappiness.

Our brain and heart conflict; we observe our feelings changing over time. Finally, we can only make an objective judgment when the relationship comes to an actual end.

My own consistency was tested by a supermarket deal I participated in last month. I was actually at the market to buy a few things. However, I couldn't resist the lure of the offer, so I decided to take advantage of the deal: earn a $15 bonus by spending $50.

When I completed my shopping in half an hour, I realized that some of the things I'd picked were not eligible. I was informed of this by the smallest fine print a person could see.

What should I do? I had made the choice to participate and already spent half an hour to find the right stuff. Leaving everything behind would mean wasting my time and missing the deal. Behaving consistently and standing behind my choice created a great deal of pressure and persuasion at the checkout. So I continued shopping to make up the missing amount with items I didn't want. All of this resulted in my buying many unwanted items to get a good deal.

As in these examples, if you can get people to stand up for an idea by leading them with the right questions, in most cases they would prefer to take action consistent with their answers under the influence of wanting to show high mental strength. In other words, their own emotions would convince them to take action. And this result will be even more powerful and lasting than any of your efforts to persuade through explanation.

To Create Effective Ground for Your Dialogues:

Do:
✓ Start by asking open-ended questions to discover commonalities and mutual interests;
✓ Ask questions regularly to make sure that the other party is listening to you and understands you;
✓ Ask questions to encourage analytical thinking and allow people to think differently.

Don't Do:
✓ Don't ask aimless questions;
✓ Don't use closed-ended questions to gather info;
✓ Being and looking consistent is crucial; do not reveal your preferences before projecting their consequences.

3. Listening to Understand

What if I play you a melody and ask you to memorize it, and then I play you a song and ask you how many times that melody occurs in the song?

It's likely that as you try to count the number of recurrences, your ability to enjoy the song and fully understand it would diminish significantly. Your brain would be occupied with the counting process and you would ignore all the other details in the song, rather like our not being able to text and drive at the same time.

Our working memory, which stores and manipulates visual images or verbal and aural information, has limited capacity. Research studies have shown that multitasking leads to as much as a 40% drop in productivity and a 10% drop in IQ.[27]

What if we turn this melody-counting exercise into a competition? Eventually, listening to the song would turn into a more anxious activity. You would notice yourself talking in your mind when you are in doubt and missing more occurrences of the melody.

Listening effectively is arduous. We think four times faster than we talk. That's why if we're not careful, we may find ourselves thinking about the past or the future while the other person is talking. Effective listening requires concentration, and concentration requires extra energy.

We make a simple and noticeable mistake: *We mainly listen to respond and usually neglect listening to understand.* When we listen to our communication partner while being carried away by our own thoughts, we miss the opportunity to more completely understand her. But we discover a completely different world when we listen effectively to someone in order to understand. We go beyond words and begin to notice needs that have not been verbalized.

For example, when men listen to women, they like to reach fast conclusions and solutions. And the women complain, "You never listen to me."

More than solutions and recommendations, women mainly want to be listened to. They expect men to be patient and listen

---

[27] "How (and Why) to Stop Multitasking"; Peter Bergman (2010)

without interrupting them, even when the subject grows complicated. Women actually wish to be valued, and the best way to show that we care for someone is by listening effectively to her.

Don't forget, *people remember others by their behaviors and by how they felt about them* (that phrase again!).

One of the main duties of the listener is to provide a comfortable environment that allows her partner to communicate easily.

Effective listening tells the other party a lot about you. If you can create a secure environment for the other person to express herself, this will inspire feelings of trust and care, which will have a more direct effect than your words. Effective listening is a powerful tool for your emotional branding.

To create a comfortable environment for communication:

- Turn your body directly towards the other party and maintain good eye contact.
- Emulate their posture, tempo, body and head movements.
- Use short phrases—interjections to create empathy and express that you understand.
- Never cut off someone speaking, though you can use short summarizing phrases regularly.
- The word "but" sends negative signals to the hearer's mind. When it's your turn to talk, never start your sentences with a "but".

The Power of Body Language in Listening

Listen to a flamenco dance video with your eyes closed. Then watch it again with your eyes open.

Which one excited you more?

Using the power of your body language as you listen to another person will also create an extensive effect for your communication, as in the flamenco dance example.

Like fine-tuning a radio frequency, we have to adjust our body language to what our communication partner does. Like watching herself in a mirror, the more she finds a resemblance between her body movements and ours, the more comfort she will feel during the conversation. The more our communication partner sees herself in us, the more comfort she'll feel.

We have to show that both our brain and our body are available during our listening.

Research shows that people who are very similar to one another unconsciously move in similar ways, as though being prompted to imitate each other by signals from their subconscious minds.

Conscious or not, imitating body language has a strong subliminal effect on our communication. As Professor Alex Matkovsky of the University of Moscow stated, our body language makes an even greater contribution to our communication than our words, even if we are only listening.

> **To Listen Effectively:**
>
> **Do:**
> - ✓ Listen to understand, not to respond;
> - ✓ Maintain good eye contact;
> - ✓ Mirror the other person's movements and posture while listening.
>
> **Don't Do:**
> - ✓ Don't cut off someone who is speaking;
> - ✓ Don't listen in order to give suggestions and advice;
> - ✓ Don't keep talking to yourself in your mind while listening.

4. Focusing on Similarities

When we buy a car or even decide on a brand, we start noticing that particular brand more and more. Similarly, when we quit our day job or start a new business, we start noticing more people with similar experiences.

In these examples, our brain plays a well-known trick on us called *selective perception*. This is our brain's tendency to highlight the information that is most relevant to us. However, we tend to interpret this to mean that there actually *are* more of the things we have begun to notice. We immediately start noticing situations that are related to us and skipping those that are not.

We tend to read and collect information that lines up with our thoughts and ignore that which does not. Similarly, we tend to like people we think are like us. We are more likely to start a relationship with someone if we agree with him and find our thoughts aligned with his.

Although this behavior seems rational, it means that we tend to ignore everyone who thinks differently and all information that does not align with our thoughts, almost as though they are a threat. This is actually our bias towards the outer world.

In their research into people's innate characteristics[28], Karen Wynn and Paul Bloom of Yale University worked with three- and five-month-old babies. The results show that we all have an innate affinity with those who make choices similar to ours, and we have punitive instincts towards those who have different preferences. The results also show that our inherited, collective subconscious plays a major role in our preferences and behaviors.

Highlighting similarities will cause us to be categorized in the same area in our partner's mind. Even by saying that you have once lived in the same area, you give the other party a subliminal message that you are both coming from similar cultures. This creates a sense of affinity. This is the main reason people regularly ask the familiar question, "Where are you from?" when they meet someone.

Using similarities as an emotional branding tool is very effective because similarities are very simple to explain by both parties.

---

[28] www.cbsnews.com/video/watch/?id=50151800n

They directly reach to your partner's mind and recall resemblances between the two of you. These resemblances create comfort and eventually help form a connection. *That connection is the most crucial step in creating your emotional brand.*

Discovering similarities stirs up feelings, opening a door for you to immediately touch some emotional strings that are linked with those similar experiences or preferences.

For example, if we find out that we are both divorced with no children, we immediately feel a part of a community. This tells us that we both have had similar experiences and consequently made similar choices. We immediately feel closer and distinguished as a part of the same community.

My most popular blog posts this year were not my best ones. People only liked my posts as much as they have found their experiences similar, or as much as they have benefited from the topics. By touching some strings and directly reaching their minds, the similarities in experiences and benefits caused the readers to recall certain feelings.

Highlighting our similarities creates a sense of belonging and sympathy. It isn't hard to see that people who focus on similarities and share stories of mutual interests demonstrate stronger communication skills than those who don't.

5. Storytelling

The main reason we like to read books and watch movies is that we like listening to stories and we like the feelings created by them.

If told well, stories stir the hearer's emotions and offer a long-lasting learning experience. Stories are powerful because people never forget how they feel. Again, more than they care about us and our words, people actually care most about how we make them feel and about the emotional value that we generate.

Another reason why we like stories is because we humans are social creatures by nature and yearn for status by spreading and sharing ideas with our peers. We feel smart and caring by sharing stories; and most times it's the best way of saying things when we have trouble saying them directly.

Telling stories not only help us create our own emotional brand but also benefits our peers by giving them a gift to be able to socialize and share the idea too. So it's a two way street for both sides benefits.

Seth Godin says, when you hear an idea from two people, it counts for twice as much as if you randomly hear it once. And if you hear an idea from ten people, the impact is completely off the charts compared to just one person whispering in your ear. (Seth Godin, Message amplification isn't linear, 2013)

Stories have a way of drawing attention, create followers, arouse curiosity, cause people to become closer and help to provide consensus.

Some stories are more successful than others because they contain a promise; they promise the audience entertainment, security or a shortcut.

Good stories are consistent within themselves and with real life, and they are unique. And they usually point to the bigger picture. Less-detailed stories are stronger if they have a way of appealing both to our emotions and logic.

And maybe most importantly, stories seek to develop awareness not by teaching something new, but by helping us rediscover what we already know. As Galileo famously said, "We cannot teach people anything; we can only help them discover it within themselves."

We should understand that preaching and giving advice do not produce results. We need to narrate topics in a way that produces empathy and makes the listener part of the story. To appeal to emotions and make people feel something, we have to make ourselves and others think multi-dimensionally by telling stories.

In his article[29] in *Brandage* magazine, author and marketing consultant Roger Dooley discussed six features of persuasive stories.

1. **Narration:** Think about a situation in which a good narrator is more persuasive than an average one. It wouldn't be wrong to say that the narration of a lawyer in the courtroom may have great influence over the verdict. A dramatic narration that is far from boring and involves asking some questions allows it to be more persuasive and catchy.

---

[29] "Six Features of Persuasive Stories"; Roger Dooley, Brandage Apr. 2013: 56.

2. **Vivid Descriptions:** As we have noted before, our brain works with visualities and categories. For example, when you close your eyes and think of "milk," you can easily visualize a milk bottle. Similarly, even if you can't recall a certain word, you can see the visual of the thing in your mind.

 When you tell a story, try using vivid descriptions that will create images and visuals in the listener's imagination. For example, when you refer to someone, don't just call him a man; describe his height, weight, age, hair color, body type or other characteristic to create visuality and evoke empathy in the listener's mind as if he is experiencing the situation himself. Brain scans have shown that when accompanied by vivid descriptions, various actions make an impact on the listener as if he is experiencing the situation himself. Now let's close your eyes and image an ant walking on a red and white checked tablecloth towards a purple jam pot. Did you see the ant in your mind's eye even if you haven't seen such an image before?

3. **Realism and Clarity:** Examples from real life, including the listener's life, always make the narration more engaging and memorable. Stories that conform to the basic motivations of people can produce empathy and are therefore more powerful.

4. **Structure:** It is important to build the progression of the story in a logical sequence and narrate by separating the story into sections. If the story is constructed incorrectly and fails to establish a logical flow of events, the influence of the story will fade even if the content stays the same.

5. **Environment:** Unsettled or noisy environments that cause the story to be interrupted frequently can reduce its credibility. In a similar way, a "pushy" narrative can decrease the story's

credibility by giving the listeners the idea that the storyteller will somehow benefit from the outcome. If I am too persistent in telling you a story that you might be reluctant to hear, you might get the idea that I will benefit from telling the story, and so it would decrease the credibility of the story.

6. **Listener Experience:** Even if you *logically* convince the audience, in order for you to be completely credible the listener must find himself in the story. He must feel like you are telling him something that he already knows but never thought about in that way.

> ### To Be Memorable and Produce Empathy:
>
> #### Do:
> ✓ Instead of giving advice, tell stories that appeal to emotions;
> ✓ Allow the other party to find himself in the story;
> ✓ Design your story well so it clearly delivers the results it promises.
>
> #### Don't Do:
> ✓ The way you narrate your story is important; don't be boring and stifling;
> ✓ Don't waste your story if the environment is not suitable for clear communication;
> ✓ Don't forget to be positive and consistent in your communication.

6. Controlling Our Emotions

Because we are under great stress in our daily lives and our time grows more valuable than ever, our brain tries to achieve a significant comfort level in every possible case.

Some people try to relax by shopping, some by sports, some by playing an instrument, but they all seek out consistency in behaviors to relax their minds.

To display consistent behaviors and be harmonious, we first have to control our emotions and then try to understand what is really happening that is stirring our emotions. Only an individual who is aware of his emotions and weaknesses can govern them and retain control of his life.

Think of someone who has a quick temper and cannot control his emotions. Can he display consistent behaviors?

If we let our emotions dominate our behaviors, then in the midst of our emotional peaks we start being delusional and start drifting away from the truth of the situation and into fallacy.

For example, an exceptionally jealous man may lose control and suddenly become furious, acting aggressively towards someone who actually was only trying to help his girlfriend. It really doesn't matter how polite or understanding he normally is, because his behaviors are not predictable and consistent.

Developing awareness and control over our emotions like anger, fear, sadness, surprise and joy is very important for our consistency.

Many things may change in life unexpectedly. If we can't control our emotions, we also can't control our behaviors; we keep losing our grip on the situations that are beyond our control. As modern men and women, we have to control our emotions in order to be consistent and successful.

In this regard we basically have two options: *either we control our emotions or our emotions control us.*

It's not realistic to say, "I will never get worried or get angry again." But developing awareness of our emotional moments is a good place to start creating alternative forms of behavior and try taking control of our feelings.

Remember that *Change requires Awareness + Action.*

For example, although we may be very tired, when we get angry we suddenly get energetic. Right at this time when our energy level climbs high, remember the importance of not allowing our emotions to rule our behaviors and try to take necessary actions to control them.

Never react instantly. As the famous quote goes, "Speak when you're angry and you'll make the best speech you'll ever regret" Otherwise, give it some time and wait at least 10 minutes before succumbing to temptation. Some alternative behaviors may be using humor or giving feedback that would produce empathy.

Take deep breaths and smile. Consciously smiling when you get angry, sad or scared is also a great way to change your mode. Psychologist Dr. Robert Zajonc, well-known for his studies on smiling, says, "Smiling works almost like a medicine on us."

Smiling causes physiological changes in the brain that cool your blood. Research proves that smiling reduces your overall levels of stress, lowers blood pressure, and helps to increase your mood. Zajonc finds that smiling releases serotonin and endorphins that act like a pain killer relaxing our mind, bringing out positive senses and providing a sense of pleasure and reward.

Glucose is the human body's key source of energy. It is also a primary source of energy for the brain, so its availability influences psychological processes. When glucose is low, psychological processes requiring mental effort (e.g., self-control, effortful decision-making) are impaired[30]. Sleeping well and exercising regularly increases glucose utilization in the brain and therefore creates a suitable environment to control ourselves and feelings.

The energy level of someone who is downhearted is very low. Her body craves foods that would release serotonin, the so-called the "happiness hormone," which generates happiness and energy. That's the reason why a sad person often feels like eating chocolate.

Think of a recent situation when you may have lost control of your emotions and acted in an undignified way.

At that moment when your emotions peaked, how did you feel?

What did you think?

What did you do?

Did anyone feel bad because of what you did or because the situation fell apart unnecessarily?

Could you have acted differently? What will you do differently if it happens again?

---

[30] *"The Physiology of Willpower: Linking Blood Glucose to Self-Control"*; Gailliot, Matthew T.; Baumeister, Roy F (2007)

Try to give answers to those questions and think how the situation would have ended up if you had controlled your emotions and behaved differently.

We can't learn to accept differences by always being with people who are like us. Try spending some time with the people you don't like or you clash with. Try to discern the reasons behind their differences. Like you do with physical workouts, hold "emotional practice sessions" in accepting differences and controlling your emotions and behaviors. In time, you may observe that you might also be doing similar irritating behaviors. Try to change your habits by observing and taking necessary actions.

To Be Consistent:

Do:
- ✓ Observe your reactions 15-20 seconds before your emotions take control of your behaviors;
- ✓ Spend time with people who think differently; have "emotional practice" sessions;
- ✓ When you calm down from an emotional peak, reassess the situation.

Don't Do:
- ✓ Do not listen to the things your emotions tell you to do;
- ✓ Don't expect a major change in your behaviors in the short run;
- ✓ Do not underestimate the positive influence smiling has on your emotional behaviors.

7. Displaying Memorable Characteristics

It is inevitable that passive and weedy people appear ineffective and "greyed out" in a crowd. After a conversation, they don't print themselves on your memory. You can't think of any particular characteristic associated with them.

Characteristics are the inherited image that gives a person his or her personality. They are the traits associated with someone, like being sage, innovative or rebellious.

Brands also try to display certain characteristics in their communication with their clients. Like people, a brand can easily be distinguished when it starts to be associated with a certain characteristic. As the brand is categorized with similar and noticeable information in consumers' minds, the brand will be much more permanent and easy to access.

The easiest way to place ourselves in a certain category in someone's mind during a conversation is by expressing ourselves with certain behaviors that recall certain characteristics, such as the 12 we'll look at in a moment. This provides a great consistency, because these characteristics directly appeal to the categories that exist in the audience's mind by using a form of language that is already known.

Every individual has distinct characteristics. If someone's characteristics and our similarities with her make us feel good and create value, then our relationship can be built on solid ground.

Margaret Mark and Carol Pearson have summed up these characteristics in 12 main categories[31]:

Magician: These are the people or brands that create magical moments. For example, athletes and well-known entrepreneurs can be acknowledged in this category. High-tech brands that lead the market with new and effective products like 3D vision or huge high-definition televisions can also be put in this category.

Explorer: The people and brands in this category are free-spirited. They embark on personal adventures to create a better world and rediscover themselves. We can put people who travel different

---

[31] *The Hero And The Outlaw: Building Extraordinary Brands Through The Power Of Archetypes;* M. Mark and C. Pearson (2001)

parts of the world to free-fall, surf or snowboard in this category. Brands in this category usually offer fast service, thrive to make difference and represent an adventurous spirit by their name and logo.

Caregiver: These people and brands have a reputation for caring for others by making them feel secure and comfortable. We can easily put doctors and nurses in this category. Also in this category would be brands that make their consumers feel valued and cared for by providing various communication platforms and providing a solution-oriented, customer-focused management style rather than creating platforms that are only for show.

Creator: Represents innovation, creativity and artistry. People in this category seek beauty and aesthetic standards, along with innovation. They are dreamers. For example, people who are into music and art can easily be put in this category. Innovative brands are mostly the ones that offer various options to their customers and provide opportunities to have their products personalized.

Ruler: People and brands that bring fundamental changes to large-scale social problems or obstacles are a part of this category. They are the ones who have proven their value and strength, and they have great tendency towards power and control. For examples, leaders who take a company or a country to a higher point may belong to this category. Brands that dominate the market and create high-level benefits can be considered as ruler brands.

Jester: They promise good times and fun. They are mostly irresponsible, cynical or cheerful. For example, comedians and humorists can be a part of this category. The companies who give life to fun cartoon heroes are the best brand ambassadors of this category.

Regular Guy/Gal: Represents the fatalistic working class, the realistic general public that doesn't expect much from life. Like a subdued family portrait, the "regular guy/gal" characteristic symbolizes an intimate and not-very-passionate structure that is satisfied with the status quo. This brand category is made for everyday use and is not expected to be innovative or passionate.

Lover: Represents sincerity, romance and especially passion. Ambassadors of this category use seduction as a tool, or even as a weapon. Famous women who are pop-culture favorites and artists who highlight their aesthetic standards are examples of this category. Car and cosmetic brands that emphasize aesthetics and passion can also be considered as lover brands.

Hero: Represents bravery and warriorship. In general, we may include inspirational athletes and influential political leaders in this group. We can consider market-leader auto and fashion brands that tenaciously try new ways to connect with their consumers to be brand ambassadors of this category.

Outlaw: They are rebellious and dissonant, they defy rules and order and they are the ones that survive. We can put most writers and actors in this category. We may also place some free-spirited motorcycle and vintage clothing brands in this category.

Innocent: Represents goodness, purity and childlike character. Ambassadors of this characteristic are modest and serene. People in this category are usually accepting. When you talk to them you can easily understand their goodness and naivety. We can place brands that emphasize goodness and purity in their ad campaigns in this category.

Sage: Represents knowledge and enlightenment. They lead their communication partners or consumers to think and to learn. They are inclined to be scientific. We can put professors, scientists and lecturers in this category. Brand ambassadors in this category would be documentary channels and television programs that aim to create a benefit by discussing important issues.

Now, which characteristics do you see yourself possessing?

The best way to answer such a question is by listening to your heart. You will find your true characteristics by thinking about who you really are instead of thinking about who you really want to be. Try to find which characteristics and behaviors you are most comfortable with.

Think about some movie stars and try to match them with the characteristics above. You will notice that they perfectly fit in some roles because they are the true representatives of certain characteristics.

Like people, brands can also showcase more than one characteristic. For example, a person can be categorized as **"Jester"** because of his cheerful and playful attitude, and also can be categorized as **"Creator"** because of the power of his imagination.

Likewise, a brand can be categorized as **"Outlaw"** by offering vintage and heavily washed products and might also be categorized as **"Explorer"** because of its ad campaigns focusing on the customer's freedom.

Let's take a look at some famous advertising brand slogans:

"The best a man can get"

"It's the real thing"

"Don't leave home without it"

Do they promise anything? Or do they just claim that they're the best or the most needed?

When we present ourselves like this, do others also categorize us the same way? Or, to make a difference and emphasize a certain characteristic, does our story ultimately need to promise a real benefit?

Let's take a look at the brand slogans below and observe which characteristics they would like to put forward:

"Makes milk fun" **(Jester** and **Innocence)**

"Wash and go" **(Caregiver** and **Explorer)**

"Have it your way" **(Creator** and **Explorer)**

If we focus on the characteristics that best express who we are, then we can display a powerful and a distinctive character model that is also easy to remember.

To stick in someone's mind, it's very important to use many communication channels simultaneously and consistently that specifically represent certain characteristics, such as appealing to certain needs, highlighting certain similarities, and maybe the most important of them all, maintaining a particular appearance that is consistent with our characteristic. This triggers the fast thinking that dominates most people's thoughts and opinions.

5

Controlling Our Behaviors

How do you want to be treated?

Always with a gentle manner and respectful behavior, right?

No one wants to be treated in a disrespectful and presumptuous manner.

Those of you who had such an experience would certainly agree with me that waiting tables actually teaches you how to treat people.

But do we ever treat others, especially the people who are closest to us, disrespectfully under the influence of our emotions?

Sometimes it's possible that we might lose our temper and break hearts unwittingly. At those times, what we want to achieve trumps how we go about achieving it. In order to reach the "what" that we have in mind, we're willing to allow all kinds of "hows".

However, leadership, one of the most popular topics of our era, reminds us that *how* we accomplish something is even more important than the goal itself.

Leadership is not just about business or politics; it's also about our personal competency to fulfill our responsibilities and lead our lives. Regardless of our position and status in life, we assume many leadership roles during the day.

There are many qualities that shape a successful leader. The most important of them are the leader's attitude, his interpersonal skills and character.

On a TV program about leadership, participants played a game that revealed the importance of applying leadership principles to our daily lives. The game's rules were simple. Each participant was given four fake gold coins (actually chocolates). Then they were asked to choose the people who had best demonstrated leadership traits during the program and award their gold coins to these participants one by one. The player who collected the most coins was the person who had acted most like a leader during the day.

The most instructive part was the interviews after the allocation of the coins. The players who gave coins to the winner were asked to explain their choices. The most common explanations focused on the winner's attitudes during the day. Some said, "I gave him my coin because I felt very comfortable speaking to him." Another said, "He was helpful to me and to others during the day," or "He managed to find time for me and listened to me carefully." Ultimately people selected this person as a leader not because of his knowledge or talents but because of his attitudes.

At the time of the 2012 U.S. presidential election, one of my friends said, "If I could vote, I would definitely vote for Obama instead of Romney." I asked her why. Her answer was very interesting. She said, "Because I feel like he will reply to me if I send him an e-mail."

She was willing to vote for him not for any political reason or anything to do with world affairs, but because of the intimacy and sincerity he managed to convey by appealing to emotions. Obama's appearance, attitude, tone of voice and posture were enough to qualify him as a leader in her eyes.

Now, think about the people you accept as natural leaders, whose ideas you respect. Do you only consider them natural leaders because of their wisdom or capabilities? Or is there something more, even if you can't pinpoint it? It may be their behaviors and attitudes which carry substantial importance and enhance their communication.

Leadership is a matter of processes, not results. And the beginning of this process is always based on dialogue, self-awareness and caring.

Leadership actually begins with managing our own selves and behaviors. People who are aware of their weaknesses and who are process- and result-oriented rather than pessimistic and irresponsible can show leadership qualities.

We can specify many traits for a leader, but we cannot easily give a basic definition of leadership, because there is not just one kind of leader. For example, Gandhi, Martin Luther King, Jr. and Hitler were all leaders, but they all had vastly different styles. You do not lead like someone else, and someone else does not lead like you.

However, we should pay special attention to a single distinction: does the leader base his leadership style on fear, or on love?

Think of yourself. How much can you internalize an idea from someone who uses fear and authority as a weapon? Would you put your best effort into it just because someone obligates you to do something? Or because you believe in the benefits of it?

Only with a leader who bases his leadership style on love will you readily take responsibility and do the job to the best of your ability, because such a leader will not only consider results but also will consider mutual interests (such as rewarding a sales team for meeting a quota) and your individual interests (such as earning a promotion).

Take the best speeches of some leaders; they all promise a benefit for the audience. Likewise, we should base our individual leadership model on appealing to mutual interests and to emotions in addition to controlling our attitudes.

Our Weaknesses and Strengths

Have you ever written down your weaknesses and strengths?

If not, take a few minutes and write down your weaknesses and strengths on a piece of paper. I strongly suggest that you write down your weaknesses, because it's easier for our brain to categorize, retain and memorize visual information.

Ask a close friend or relative to help you discover your blind spots, those behaviors that you are blind to but others can see. Blind spots can include losing your temper easily, experiencing social phobia, being perfectionistic and being impatient.

Be honest with yourself, and do this for your own good. Then, during conversations, try to recall your weaknesses and your strengths so you can consciously take control of your behaviors.

After any situation where your emotions have taken control of your behaviors, try to remember the responses of your body 15 to 20 seconds before your emotional peaks. Next time when your emotions begin to come to the surface, take deep breaths and smile.

Try to control your emotions by recalling your weaknesses and the consequences of your previous actions. And try focusing on logical solutions instead of rushed actions. Don't expect sudden changes; keep working on this and try to improve yourself gradually.

For example, when you feel jealousy taking over and feel that your emotion is starting to dominate your behaviors, try to interject your logic. The picture that's taking shape in your head may be much different from the reality. Doubt and concern cause anger, and anger pulls you away from reality.

In such situations, the best thing that you can do is to start a conversation and to give feedback, highlighting the points that are upsetting you. Also try to increase your confidence by recalling your strengths (which you have previously written down).

You can also create self-awareness by keeping a list of different situations when your emotions take over.

List the reason it happened, as well as the consequences of those moments. As you keep writing down your exact feelings during these incidents and observe similarities between them, you will also start to discover the reasons or situations that cause your emotions to shine. Maybe you'll notice a past event from your family history or from the environment you've lived in that you frequently refer to.

Creating such self-awareness will provide you with a great starting point to acknowledge your weak points and start working on controlling your emotions. As we have stated earlier, your awareness will start working like a medicine to slowly change your behaviors.

To Demonstrate Leadership Qualities:

Do:
- ✓ Write down and memorize your weaknesses and strengths;
- ✓ Focus on mutual benefits and value people;
- ✓ Observe your reactions when your emotions start to take over, and develop logical counter -reactions to achieve control of your emotions.

Don't Do:
- ✓ Don't try to stand out from the crowd intentionally; let people do it for you;
- ✓ Don't manage your relationship with fearsome attitudes;
- ✓ Don't think that you are indispensable just by relying on your wisdom and competencies.

Relational Leadership

Relational leadership is essentially a kind of situational leadership. It refers to *valuing other people's strengths and working with people and through people to achieve win – win results.* A relational leader is the person who is aware of others' competencies and strengths. She aims to value people and get optimum results by stepping forward when she is capable and leading others to step forward when she is not.[32]

At first glance, leadership can be seen as managing or directing a group of people. However, real success comes from encouraging and allowing others to take responsibility when they have the improved knowledge and ability to lead in the given situation.

For example, have you ever wondered how the Internet started?

The Internet first emerged as a result of a group of people with different purposes and motivations all working together. The participants, who had never met each other but believed in the benefits of the project, started to join the growing network of computers by all leading their own projects and showing individual leadership profiles to do so. Finally, with many more people joining the network, the Internet reached its present state.

Since childhood we have been expected to be our best. Being second in a race or getting an average grade on an exam was always considered insufficient. You might have seen someone bewail getting an A- instead of an A+.

Trying to be perfect at all times is wearing, and it also wears on the people around us. It leads us to struggle for the approval and appreciation of others.

---

[32] *Primal Leadership: Realizing the Power of Emotional Intelligence*; Boyatzis, R.E., Goleman, D., McKee, A. Boston: Harvard Business School Press (2002)

Take TV ratings, for example. Is it a failure to come in second in the ratings? Or is it the program's success in appealing to diverse cultures and being talked about that really matters?

The constant struggle to come first and the addiction for approval eventually lead a person to ignore his own needs as well as others'. By trying to be the leader at all times, one can only position himself as a troublemaker and a follower, because his own individual greed will trump group interests. People will quit seeing him as a natural leader, as they won't feel comfortable with someone who doesn't pay attention to their needs.

Constant leadership breeds addiction to constant approval. Leadership means walking together, not ahead. A good leader listens and values; he strengthens personal relationships.

Everyone has different and distinct ways of doing things. A good leader respects this and tries to take advantage of this by empowering people. It's also crucial to be able to take a step back when needed. Relational leadership improves morale by allowing people to feel valued.

Our Attitude and Reactions

Teacher and author Charles Swindoll has said, "Life is 10% what happens to you and 90% how you react to it." Indeed, life is a process of actions and reactions.

For example, anger is always secondary; being hurt always comes first. You can see this in arguments between husbands and wives. The wife will say, "Why are you getting angry?" The husband will reply, "You say that as if I'm getting angry for no reason!" For the couple to reach a solution, it's important to find out the main cause of the injury in the first place instead of trying to figure out who is right or who is wrong.

Think of a situation where you reacted under the influence of your feelings, and subsequent actions and reactions caused the situation to get out of control. It's common in such situations for both parties to drift away from the actual problem.

How was your attitude in that situation?

How might the situation have ended if you had reacted differently? Can you say you or the others around you would hurt less if you were to react differently?

Our attitudes and reactions arise from how we interpret the world. Our interpretations can be completely different from reality. When our interpretation doesn't match the reality, our reactions may be very different from how we would normally react to that specific situation. This will trigger reactions in others, and ultimately this chain of actions and reactions will go on and on.

For instance, let's say that you call one of your friends on the phone but don't reach him. An hour later you try again. Still no answer. Two days pass. Your friend doesn't call you back, even though it's been two days.

How would you interpret this?

Some people might interpret this situation as, "He doesn't value me; if he did, he would have called me back within two days." Let's call these people **Group A**.

Others might say, "I must have done something bad to upset him. I think he doesn't answer my calls because of my behavior the other day." Let's call those people **Group B**.

And a third group might respond, "He must be really busy. I hope it's not a health issue." Let's call those people **Group C**.

As you can see, we have three different—but equally likely—interpretations for the same situation. Now, let's talk about the reaction of each group.

People who belong to **Group A** might say, "If he doesn't care about me, I don't care about him." They most probably would be upset and feel "put out" by their friend. They wouldn't answer the phone even if he called back.

People in **Group B** would continue blaming themselves and show timid and anxious behaviors. Most likely, the reason for their reactions would never be understood by the other side, and this would lead to a series of events, eventually resulting in a loss of communication.

The people who belong to **Group C** would call their friend back to check whether everything is all right. Even if they still can't reach him, they would leave a message to show that they care and are worried about him.

Each reaction will start a new chain of reactions, each side responding to the actions of the other according to his own interpretations.

People act like a mirror, first interpreting the image and then reflecting it through reactive behaviors. In the short run, the best thing we can do to demonstrate leadership qualities, and for our happiness, is to control our reactions and adopt our best attitude, not letting our interpretations be influenced by our emotions. In the long run, our experiences with people will show us their actual intentions, so that we can shape our choices and decisions accordingly.

I have always found Charles Plumb's story[33] about attitudes very instructive.

Plumb was a U.S. Navy jet pilot in the Vietnam War. After 75 combat missions, his plane was hit by a rocket, and he parachuted onto enemy soil in 1967. He was captured and spent six years in a Vietnamese prison. After he returned home, Plumb started lecturing on the lessons he had learned from that experience.

One day, when Plumb and his wife were sitting in a restaurant, a man from another table walked over and said, "You're Plumb! You flew jet fighters in Vietnam from the aircraft carrier Kitty Hawk. You were shot down!"

This man was the sailor who had packed Plumb's parachutes. He was the man responsible for his surviving the jump. Although Plumb might have seen him many times on board he had never acknowledged him before, not even to say, "Good morning, how are you?" Plumb explains, "Because, you see, I was a fighter pilot and he was just a sailor."

Now in his lectures Plumb asks his audience, "Who's packing your parachute?"

We always have people "packing our chute" to help us make it through the situations we encounter each day. We may fail to show an attitude of gratitude to them, preferring in most cases to

---

[33] www.axpow.org/stories-whopacksyourparachute.htm

just complain or take things for granted. However, those people at least deserve words like *hello, please*, or *thank you*. They deserve to be congratulated or to be given a compliment, or be shown extra kindness for no special reason.

Start changing your attitude towards the people around you, whether they pack your chute or not. You will notice that your life will change in a positive way, because life is a simple process of actions and reactions all the way.

6

Building Empathy

We can briefly define empathetic communication as getting in the shoes of the other person and trying to interpret the situation through his perspective. In this communication process, we need to show the other side that we not only understand his thoughts but also understand his feelings about the situation.

To be able to build empathy, we first need to accept the fact that the other side has a unique identity just as we do, and he might have different values and beliefs[34]. In this regard, we need to make an effort to completely understand the other side before judging him good or bad or right or wrong.

Okay, but how can we best understand the state of the other party—by our never-ending criticism? Or by starting a dialogue and asking questions to comprehend the situation first?

Let's consider this exchange that I witnessed some time ago.

It was a bright Sunday morning, with no clouds to block the sun shining all the way up. I caught the 10:15 ferry that sails straight across the Bosporus. Like most people, I preferred to sit outside as the weather was gorgeous. Two elderly ladies sat beside me and across from me was a mom in her thirties with her young son. After a short chat, one of the older women next to me turned to the boy, who was looking pretty unhappy, and asked him his name.

The boy replied with a reluctant and weak voice, "Andrew..."

"What a beautiful name. I also have a grandson called Andrew. How old are you?" asked the other lady.

Again with utmost reluctance the boy replied, "Nine..."

The ladies, who realized that they would not get much attention from the boy, turned to his mother instead. "You have a very nice boy, and he is very timid like my grandson. Did you also separate from your husband like my daughter?"

The boy's mother nodded faintly, but it was obvious that she didn't want to talk at all.

At last, the ladies understood that the conversation wouldn't be going anywhere, so between themselves they started to criticize the situation. "This divorce process mostly affects children. I also told my daughter that marriage is not child's play. As usual she resisted. Times have changed; now the new generation is very impatient and combative. If they can't get what they want, they immediately decide to get a divorce."

During this exchange, I noticed the woman across from me growing tired and feeling bored.

---

[34] *Empathy in the Context of Philosophy*, Lou Agosta, Palgrave/Macmillan, 2010

The final question posed to the young mother revealed the true face of the situation.

One of the elderly ladies asked her, "Did you really try? I mean, look at this poor boy. My daughter has made the same mistake. Couldn't you work things out?"

The young woman couldn't hold back any longer. With quiet intensity she said, "We didn't get a divorce. My husband passed away three months ago."

Silence prevailed.

The elderly lady couldn't find anything to say but a weakly mumbled condolence. I didn't hear much from the ladies beside me after that.

So, let's examine the situation. Was the old lady who was trying to give advice just prejudiced or bad-intentioned?

Or, when she heard the boy's name was Andrew, did her mind momentarily go to the category that includes the distress of her grandson, and with a protective instinct she felt the urge to give the same suggestions to the mother?

The old ladies had come to a fast conclusion through their own experiences. They filled in the rest of the story by relying on the information in their minds without understanding the real feelings and facts behind the situation. The real story turned out to be completely different.

Another communication pitfall we encounter is the *individuality paradox*, valuing the feelings of the people who are emotionally close to us more than the feelings of others.

Let's observe this through an example of a mother expressing opinions about her children's lives.

A neighbor asks, "How's your son?"

Mom replies, "He has a rough marriage. He wakes up early in the morning, makes his own breakfast before leaving for work. I know his wife never helps him. Can you imagine, his wife getting up an hour after he leaves home?"

"How's your daughter?"

"Thank God, she is very happy. She has a great husband who takes care of her. I heard that he wakes up an hour before my daughter and prepares breakfast for her before leaving home. My son-in-law is an angel."

Here, we can easily see that the mother has a personal perspective that favors her children, although both cases are more or less the same. However, to be able to create a healthy, emphatic communication environment, we need to be objective towards each party in the situation.

Not favoring the people that we feel close to is difficult because of the impact of emotions on our decisions and behaviors. We need to do it, however, in order to build our own sound emotional branding. It would be wise to double-check our interpretations by changing our perspective in each situation.

For Empathetic Communication:

Do:
✓ Ask questions in order to better understand the situation and the emotions of the other party;
✓ Be respectful of different values and beliefs;
✓ Make an extra effort to place yourself in the picture.

Don't:
✓ Don't judge;
✓ Don't advise;
✓ Don't jump to conclusions based on your past experiences.

The Johari Window

The Johari Window[35] is a model developed in 1995 by Joseph Luft and Harry Ingram that helps an individual to explain his relationships with others and himself. It consists of four sections

---

[35] "The Johari Window, a graphic model of interpersonal awareness"; Luft, J.; Ingham, H. Los Angeles: UCLA (1955)

that each describe what he and others know or don't know about him.

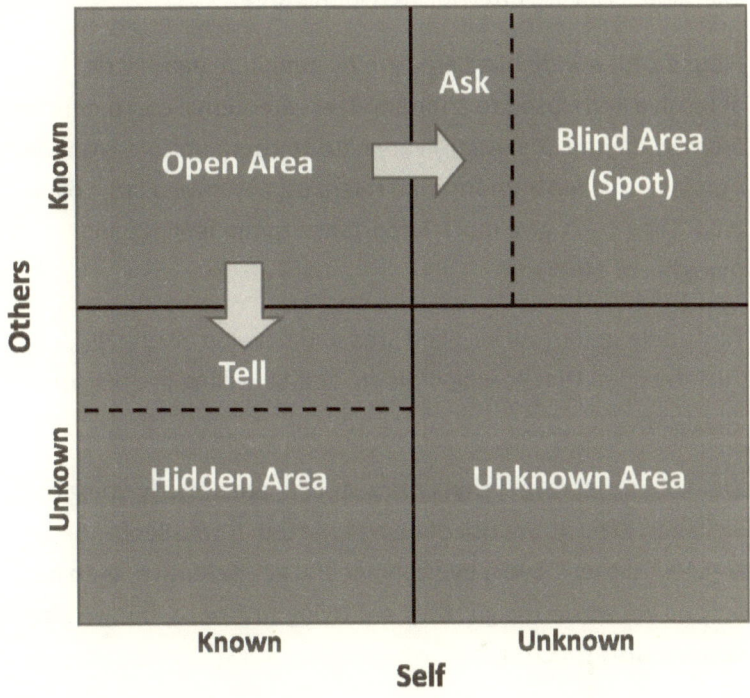

Open Area: This area involves the individual's personal traits and behaviors that are known by both the individual himself and others. In general, this area comprises information that one does not hesitate to tell and that can be easily observed by others.

People with a large open area can communicate very easily. They are comfortable, confident individuals with well-developed emotional competencies. This type of person has a strong ability to empathize. They care about other people's thoughts and feelings, accept differences and diversity and they are open to cooperation and sharing ideas.

Blind Area: Represents the area of oneself that he cannot see but which can be observed by others. Feelings like anxiety, fear, envy and skepticism are often located in this area.

People with a wide blind area are by definition egocentric, defensive and closed to criticism. Their emotional competencies are very limited. It's usually very hard to communicate with them. Domineering and authoritarian rulers usually have a large blind area. They don't give much importance to the feelings and thoughts of others.

To be able to narrow his blind area and develop awareness, one must be open to receiving criticism and be willing to ask a lot of questions.

We must never forget that critical people are actually doing us a big favor, even at the risk of being rejected. If we silence them, argue with them, avoid eye contact and get defensive, then not only do we waste the gift they are trying to give us, but we also become disrespectful.

Virgin Group CEO Richard Branson says that one of the main reasons his business succeeded in a short time is that he asked plenty of questions. Branson says, "I was willing to listen to anyone who could help, and over the years many people volunteered their advice."

Hidden Area: This area includes features that are known by the person himself but not by others. It consists of the information one does not want to share and deliberately hides from others.

People with a wide hidden area are timid and usually have social phobia. They dislike seeking their rights, taking risks and ambiguity. It's also hard to communicate with these people. They can take criticism but cannot criticize. They prefer to ignore and escape from problems.

To narrow this area and develop awareness about himself, one must not be afraid to talk about his qualities and his thoughts. He needs to get over his shyness.

Unknown Area: This area includes subconscious behaviors that are unknown to the individual himself and also cannot be explained by others. We can say that very young people and the elderly tend to have wide unknown areas.

People with a wide unknown area are prescriptive and frosty. They can't explain most of their behaviors and don't want to question, either. They mostly conceal their thoughts and behaviors and avoid conflicts.

Someone who wants to improve his innovation and creativity should make an effort to narrow this area. To do so, he is advised to develop self-esteem by attempting new things and doing things at which he is likely to succeed. In this way, he can explore and demonstrate qualities that even he is not aware he had.

In the Johari Window, the areas may vary according to the different roles we possess during our daily routines. Thoughts, feelings and observations can shift easily from one area to another.

For our emotional branding, we mostly need to develop our open area, and the best way to enhance it is by taking and giving feedback in the right way.

For Empathetic Communication:

Do:
- ✓ Ask questions in order to better understand the situation and the emotions of the other party;
- ✓ Be respectful of different values and beliefs;
- ✓ Make an extra effort to place yourself in the picture.

Don't:
- ✓ Don't judge;
- ✓ Don't advise;
- ✓ Don't jump to conclusions based on your past experiences.

Criticizing and Giving Feedback

It does not matter how open minded we think we are about being criticized, most of us feel bad. A part of us feels hurt and needs to get defensive when we are criticized.

Did you ever consider the main reason behind our negative feelings towards criticism?

This sentiment in fact stems from our inner 'expectant parent voice'[36]. When you received your first report card from school, do you remember how you felt in front of your parents, who were expecting an A+ instead of a B+? Do you recall how you felt when you were questioned about your average grades although you had many A's along with them?

That felt very bad, right?

Can we say that the behavior of our parents was bad-intentioned?

No, of course not. Maybe they only wanted to push us a little bit more or just wished us to be better than we were. But in doing so, they unintentionally placed us in a state of comparison, questioning rather than valuing what we had already accomplished.

Now whenever we are criticized or need to criticize, similar incidents come to mind. No matter how constructive the criticism is, it feels bad. Most of the time we might refrain from giving or receiving criticism. In fact, most of the things we feel during criticism are about our past experiences. They substantially evoke the feelings of similar occasions in the past.

Judith E. Glaser and Richard D. Glaser (Ph.D. in Biochemistry) from The CreatingWE Institute says, "When we face criticism, rejection or fear, when we feel marginalized or minimized, our bodies produce higher levels of cortisol, a hormone that shuts down the thinking center of our brains and activates conflict aversion and protection behaviors. We become more reactive and sensitive. We often perceive even greater judgment and negativity than actually exists. And these effects can last for 26 hours or more,

---

[36] Dr. Alp Karaosmanoğlu, Psychotherapy and Education Center

imprinting the interaction on our memories and magnifying the impact it has on our future behavior. Cortisol functions like a sustained-release tablet – the more we ruminate about our fear, the longer the impact" (Judith E. Glaser and Richard D. Glaser, The Neurochemistry of Positive Conversations, 2014)

Apart from the chemistry that plays a big role in this phenomenon, the 'expectant parent voice' is actually the main reason behind almost all our fears and doubts. When we are giving feedback, what we need to accomplish is to help the other side to focus on our feedback instead of this voice in his head.

But how?

When we are criticizing someone or giving feedback, what are the most important things we should we pay attention to?

The first rule we have to understand is that the person you criticize or give feedback to does not care much about what you think or how you feel (unless of course there is supervising involved). His primary concern is your fact-based analysis rather than your superficial thoughts.

To give effective and constructive criticism, you should mainly focus on three factors:

1. **Situation:** Be specific about where, when and during what occasion the situation took place. Give feedback with detailed explanations. As in storytelling, help the other person visualize himself in the situation. Use clear expressions to avoid any question marks. Don't just say, "The other night, in front of the building..." Say, "On Friday night, while we were leaving work with Mark through the front door..." You may use closed-ended

questions to help the other party recall the exact time and place of the situation himself.

2. **Behavior:** Be specific about the behavior that causes the problem. Do not label the person, label the behavior. Avoid generalizations. Do not use sobriquets like brother, dude, bro or sweetheart, as they would distract the other party's focus on the subject; help the person concentrate on his behavior alone. For example, while giving feedback to someone who enters your room without permission, it would be wise to begin with vivid descriptions of similar behavior that occurred previously. Calling him rude or careless would be generalizing, and he will likely get defensive instead of focusing on his behaviors.

3. **Effect:** This is the most important part of our feedback. How did the other side's behavior affect us or others? Build empathy by emphasizing the effects of the behavior. For instance, think about the person who enters your room without permission. Emphasize the consequences of his behavior by telling him how late you got home or how you missed a meeting or entered the meeting without adequate preparation. This would lead the other person to produce empathy regarding a similar experience of his.
It's important to highlight the results of his behavior rather than criticizing the person.

While criticizing someone and/or giving feedback, it is very important to pay attention to the following points:

• If possible, give two or three chances before you criticize.

• Action breeds reaction. Make sure your criticism does not include passive-aggressive behaviors and/or harsh labels.

- Try to deliver the messages by asking questions. It is the best way to create awareness and appeal to the subconscious mind and achieve behavioral changes.

- Communicate your criticism in a private place and while the situation is still fresh.

Feedback is not necessarily negative. Also share positive feedback whenever possible. If we want people to listen to us and value our thoughts, we need to show them that we also value them. If a person likes you or believes that your thoughts are similar to his, he will be more willing to listen to your criticism and feedback when the time comes.

The Power of "Reason Why"

An experiment conducted by social psychologist Ellen Langer in 1979 reveals that the word "because" is a strong and magical word in our lives.

In the experiment, a volunteer asked the people waiting in line to use a copier, "I only have five pages to copy. May I use the copy machine? Because I am in a real rush."

Ninety-four percent of the people complied with his request.

Langer repeated the experiment in another line.

But this time the volunteer asked, "I only have only five pages to copy. May I use the copy machine?"

In this case only 60% of the people complied.

Langer repeated the experiment one more time, but this time the volunteer only asked, "May I use the copy machine?" then added a meaningless phrase, "because I have to make copies."

Although the reason was meaningless, 93% of the people complied with his request.

This clearly shows us that even if the reason we bring forward in our statements is not strong, the "reason why" manages to have an unconscious influence over the listener's brain. In such cases, we tend to believe that we just need to know the reason before we will act. The "reason why" by itself becomes a great influence, even though it may not make any sense at all.

However, the explanation provided in the first situation may cause the people in the line to feel an even stronger empathy if the question were followed by something like, "...Because I am in a real rush and I have to catch the bus." In this case, the volunteer provides a vivid explanation that allows the people in line to be able place themselves in the picture. Thus, people who experienced similar situations before would recall this situation and should be more willing to comply with the volunteer.

While using the "reason why" influence in our feedback analysis, choosing reasons which the other party may have experienced before will help us evoke empathy more easily and permanently.

Highlighting mutual life experiences will appeal to the appropriate category in the listener's brain and activate his visual activity area, producing a vivid image of the possible consequences of the situation he may have experienced before. This will help the other person to envision your story and help you appeal to his emotions.

The manner in which we say "because" is as important the reason we give. In order not to distract the listener from his focus on your story, the reason you give has to be free of all positive and negative comments and passive-aggressive behaviors, just as in giving feedback.

To Give Constructive Feedback:

Do:
- ✓ Give information (analysis) not advice;
- ✓ Focus on the consequences of the behavior;
- ✓ Be very specific about the fault.

Don't Do:
- ✓ Don't intend to change the other person;
- ✓ Don't include personal pronouns and positive and negative comments in your feedback;
- ✓ Never generalize.

7

Being Passionate

We all are actually born with great enthusiasm and passion. We can observe a child playing with his toys all day long with the passion of Picasso creating his paintings or Mozart composing his music.

We can also see children asking endless questions. They are hungry for learning and foolish enough to question everything. Every child has a great passion to learn and imagine, just as we once did when we were kids.

But you might also observe most parents quell their kids or turn a deaf ear to them when children start asking questions. By their doing so, the child eventually stops asking questions and becomes an individual who categorizes questioning as inappropriate.

His subconscious always reminds him that the activity of asking questions is wrong. The parental voice succeeds in diminishing the courage and the will to question the unknown.

Now we can look at ourselves and think that we lost our passion and excitement along the way, and that the fire is extinguished. However, none of these implications is true.

Our passion still exists somewhere inside us, and it is still our most powerful weapon. It has only been suppressed over time by our fears and our inner 'expectant parental voice'. We need to acknowledge that it will never be possible to reach the safe and passionate area beyond our fears and concerns unless we face our fears and turn down the volume of this inner parental voice.

Maya Penn is a young entrepreneur, cartoonist and designer who started her first company when she was eight years old. She was ten years old when Forbes magazine contacted her to feature her and her company in an article; and she gave her first TED Talk when she was 13, after which people stood and applauded for several minutes.[37]

In contrast to Maya's experience, we tend to think that to have such a career record we must live life sitting behind a desk, calculating what we can do to refine our skills. Instead of letting our passion lead us, we prefer chasing the most reputable universities and highest-paying jobs, dreaming of giving a TED Talk someday and believing that this is the only way to do it. But trying to create the perfect resume would further succeed in killing our passion if it's being done for the wrong reasons.

According to a study[38] conducted by Prof. Jean M. Twenge and Michigan University, the number of people who say they would prefer to live a wealthy life rather than a meaningful one has risen around 30% over the last 40 years. When asked about their main purpose in life, more and more people every day will say, "I want to be rich and prosperous."

---

[37]www.ted.com/talks/maya_penn_meet_a_young_entrepreneur_cartoonist_designer_activist.html

Do you think it would be wrong to interpret this answer as, "I'm scared of being poor and unsuccessful" because our inner "expectant parental voice" whispers to us that being unsuccessful is not an option?

Sustainable success is all about putting our passion and focus into the *process* rather than focusing on the results. It is about doing them just for the sake of doing them, not because of the results we or others expect. It's about being ready to face any risks, failures or rejections in the pursuit of our passions.

Because of this fear of failure, it's as though we are constantly traveling on a city bus which is driven by a driver other than us. In public transportation, in the event of an accident we can retreat by putting all the responsibility on the driver. Likewise, we wouldn't have any concerns about the repair of the vehicle.

In the same way, we are living our lives under the control of others and are unwilling to take any risks. And by doing this, we have no choice but to go the same direction as everyone else.

Let's take a look at examples of some famous people before they reached success.

Stephen King received so many rejections for his first novel, *"Carrie"*, that in *"On Writing"* he says, "The nail in my wall would no longer support the weight of the rejection slips impaled upon it. So, I replaced the nail with a spike."

---

[38] "Generational Differences in Young Adults' Life Goals, Concern for Others, and Civic Orientation"; 1966–2009

Later, when *"Carrie"* was first published in 1974, the first print run sold around 30,000 copies.[39]

Clint Eastwood had been told that he could never be a movie star because he has a very large Adam's apple.

A modeling agency advised Marilyn Monroe to get married or to get a secretarial job because she had no future in show business.

In 1962 The Beatles were turned down by a recording company because bands with guitars were "on their way out."

Jimmy Wales was the founder of a free Internet encyclopedia he called *Nupedia*. When Wales first presented *Nupedia*, the idea was widely accepted. When he asked people if they would join such a platform, all he received were positive replies. But Wales didn't quit trying until he found a working platform: the free online encyclopedia we know as Wikipedia.

You may have read that some of the world's most successful music groups started in their garages playing awful songs. With making music as their only motivation, these people learned to write good songs by failing over and over again.

So, to be successful, do you think we need just our sheer desire to succeed? Or, like those music groups, do we need to find things that excite us and that we will do just for the purpose of doing them?

Consider those people who've had many rejections but still follow their dreams that they truly believe in. Only the things that arouse

---

[39] *Stephen King from A to Z: An Encyclopedia of His Life and Work,* George W. Beahm (1998)

our excitement and passion have the potential to eventually make us achieve exceptional results like no one else can.

Tenacity

Have you ever trained in martial arts?

I have been training in many disciplines since the age of 16. Above them all, with over 14 years of training, Muay Thai, also known as Thai Boxing, has kept me busy but set my mind free the most by far.

At the age of 20, it started as a curiosity and a need for self-defense, but later it turned into a life style. In Muay Thai, you start to feel the joy of seeing your mistakes instantly as you feel that knuckle on your chin if you lower your arm a bit.

You start being proud of doing better and better with each training session. And if you train long enough, you find yourself in a human chess game where your biggest opponent is your own fears and temper.

If you lose your temper, you lose the bout. If you maintain it but let fear take over, or you don't have the determination to win, you lose again. There is a very thin line between maintaining your state of mind and losing it. It's not just a physical bout but also a mental bout.

Even if you just start doing Muay Thai as a physical activity, if you train long enough and hard enough you start thinking about getting into tournaments to try yourself out. Well, the pride of training for a Muay Thai bout is just incredible. However, for a man who has also set his mind to being well-educated and well-rounded, the ring is not a place to call home.

From the moment you set foot in the arena on fight day, excitement and fear start to overflow and emotions starts to peak. You try to calm yourself down by recalling your long hours of regular training. And when the time comes and the lights go out for you to walk to the ring, you just try to relax and remember one thing: your own strategy. At that moment nothing remains but feelings.

And the ring…it's the loneliest place in the world. Across the ring is a man who has trained the best he could to knock you down. But the bout actually starts before the bell. It starts when both fighters set foot in the ring, because there the real bout takes place—between you and your feelings. If you let your emotions take over, you have lost already. So, at those moments I smile and try to concentrate on my own strengths instead of focusing on my opponent.

If you free your mind and focus on your strengths, only then can you control your actions. Otherwise fear and doubt take over, and it means that you have lost already.

And after the fight, you feel, *There is nothing I can't do if I set my mind to it.*

There are three reasons why I consider my Muay Thai training to be one of the things that best prepared me for life:

1. When you train for a fight, **you train with your team.** It's mostly up to those people that you train with whether you lose or win. They are the ones who push you to your limits, not because they hate you but because they love you and want to

get the most out of you. Consider them the people you work with or you are in a relationship with; if you ignore those people, train alone or don't listen to their criticism and feedback, the ring will be a much lonelier place.

2. **You learn winning by losing.** Muay Thai gives you the courage to keep trying until you succeed. Like in life, there are hard times, heartaches, headaches, knock-downs and bruises, but you see that without learning those hard lessons, you won't learn success either. Each and every time you fall, it's the tenacity to get up again that matters.

3. **It's not only about fighting** or achieving results; it's about who you become in achieving them. Controlling your emotions in a bout, getting up after a knock-down, learning lessons from the punches you receive all might sound rather brutal or not useful in a business environment, but believe me, they have proven to be tremendously useful in a business environment. It's your state of mind that makes you successful in any struggle, whether it's physical or mental. Winning is all about your self-awareness and confidence rather than who your opponent is or what the situation is.

There is nothing you cannot achieve in this world if you dream and create excitement about it. But even if you create work that has great potential, it's vital to stay positive, since you might be rejected many times before you create that excitement.

To succeed, being sustainable carries a lot more importance than sheer hard work. If you're a billiards player, you need to be up at five o'clock every day to make a thousand strokes. And when your hand bleeds you need get it fixed and return to the table for a thousand more.

On top of that, you will feel fear and doubt on your way because of the rejection that you will receive occasionally. But you should never forget that only the ones who do not quit dreaming and working can achieve great results at the end.

It's a fact that you will receive "no" as an answer many times in your life.

What "no" can mean:

- I'm too busy.
- I don't trust you.
- My boss won't let me.
- I'm not the person to decide this.
- I'm not the kind of person that does things like this.
- Doing this will cause me to do more things that I just don't want to deal with.

What "no" doesn't mean:

- I see the world the way you do, I have carefully considered every element of this proposal and understand as well as you do and I hate it and I hate you. (Seth Godin, what-no-means, 2013)

As Professor Abdul Kalam, who served as the 11th President of India, said, NO actually means the Next Opportunity.

The most effective way to get around "no" is to demonstrate stability and tenacity. And tenacity differs from persistence. Persistent people cook the same dish over and over again and expect us to eat it. However, tenacious people always try new ways to reach their goals by replacing old and ineffective ideas with new ones. People making sales calls are persistent, but brands that always try new marketing channels to attract customers are tenacious.

Did you ever wonder why people like to watch athletes?

Because tenacity, discipline and hard work attract attention and create admiration.

The only way to make changes in our general behaviors is by developing awareness of our automatic and emotional behaviors and by taking deliberate actions to lower their influence.

To change your habits, try to set realistic goals. Write them down to create visualization and place them in your subconscious. Try repeating them over and over again whenever possible. In this way your subconscious mind will work to carry you to your goals by generating new ways of doing things even while you are asleep. This will also affect the way you see things in your daily life. Your subconscious mind will begin to interpret things that you see or hear in such a way that you can use them in achieving your goals.

Ultimately, your mind will work to produce new ways to reach your goals. Putting them into practice will cause you to be perceived as a tenacious person.

To Be Passionate and Tenacious:

Do:
- ✓ Face your fears;
- ✓ Do things that excite you and that you believe can make a difference;
- ✓ Write down your goals and place them in your subconscious by repeating them.

Don't Do:
- ✓ Never get tired of the negative responses or feedbacks and most importantly never quit trying;
- ✓ Don't take heed to any negative comment that is not based on an analysis;
- ✓ Being persistent and tenacious are different; don't cook the same meal and serve it over and over again.

Self-Confidence and Motivation

When we are asked to write positive and negative things about us, it always takes us much less time to come up with the negative responses. In fact, we are so good at finding our negativities that most of the time we don't even realize when our responses are being negative.

However, in order to overcome the negative responses of others, first we need to believe in ourselves and our strengths. We need to be using confidence and motivation tools effectively in order to achieve our goals.

Our motivation is our strength and ability to overcome the obstacles on our way to success without amplifying their weight in our mind.

For example, a motivated salesperson always accepts today's negative responses with an open mind, knowing that he has the ability to overcome them in the future by the lessons learned.

Likewise, a high school boy who confidently talks to girls distinguishes himself from the crowd by having the belief that, after several attempts, he can finally turn the negative responses to positive.

Whereas it takes great self-confidence to approach girls and talk to them in high school, in time it becomes normal as our experience increases and the way we interpret life changes. Someone who interprets life more realistically even in high school will be considered as someone with high self-confidence. Self-confidence is related to how much we let our fears conquer us and how we position ourselves in our minds.

In daily life, people prefer to work and build relationships with others who have self-esteem. Self-confident and determined people who know what they want from life are reminiscent of successful people and can be categorized in the same area in our brains. Therefore, these people begin their emotional communication one step ahead of others. They appeal to emotions even with their presence.

In this struggle of life, the only person that you can trust to ensure your confidence is yourself. No one can perceive what you want to achieve as much as you can because of differences in upbringing, fears, habits and subconscious mind. You will only lose time and effort by relying on others to motivate you. It is extremely important that you know what you want out of life and that you have the ability to motivate yourself constantly.

Do you sometimes feel that your motivation is low, and so you feel the need to motivate yourself?

Find something that you're afraid of and try doing it. Nothing can motivate you as much as the experience you gain by facing your fears.

Think about what motivates you to work.

Money? A title? Are these the things that *really* motivate you to work? Or are they actually your fears of becoming unsuccessful and poor that are spurred by your inner 'expectant parent voice'?

Despite their wealth, many wealthy people are not content. They may have larger homes and cars, but they also have bigger reasons to be unhappy.

We should note that complex systems tend to break down quicker. Binding happiness into complex relationships is no different than hanging by a thread, because the bond can break at any moment with the changing balance of interests. The only luxury of the rich is that they may camouflage their unhappiness with money.

Just think, what would you really like to accomplish in life if there were no expectations upon you to earn money?

Is making more money really a criterion for success? Do you sometimes measure your success by comparing your annual income to that of others?

Sometimes, we may find ourselves complaining, "He gets fifteen dollars an hour, and I'm still at ten."

Why is it so important how much money we make today?

First of all we need to find out what we really want to do with our lives and acquire a life purpose. The real question we should be asking ourselves is, "Do I have a life purpose that excites me? Am I trying to change my habits accordingly?"

If you have a purpose in life and you train yourself in order to achieve it, it really doesn't matter who earns what. By pursuing your life's purpose, you actually make the best investment in both your future and your happiness. No one can compete with the kind of motivation that is fostered by your purpose in life.

Unfortunately we're all taking our cues from others today. We spend our lives chasing the goals and meeting the expectations of others. It always feels easier to follow someone else's dreams rather than our own. In the end we turn into individuals who have everything, but who are not ourselves. Deep inside, we are not happy because of the artificial motivations we try to find contentment with.

Our inner "expectant parent voice" constantly whispers to us that failure is graceless and not an option. This voice is the biggest of all the hurdles we face on our way to success. We will not be able to get to the safe and prosperous area beyond our fear barrier if we cannot turn down the authority of this voice in our head.

We need to create a vision of our purpose in our head and place ourselves in that vision. Only then can we wake up each morning with an energizing motivation that will distinguish us from the crowd.

After retiring from body building and embarking on an acting career in 1976, Arnold Schwarzenegger appeared in the movie "Stay Hungry". The film was derided as a complete disaster, but in an interview to publicize the movie, Arnold said these words: "I'm going to be the number one box-office star in all of Hollywood."

Many people were skeptical about him after this interview, and with good reason. The movie didn't hold much promise. It was also not very convincing for someone in his twenties from Austria, with a distinct Austrian accent, to come to the U.S. and say that he wants to be a star in Hollywood. Moreover, unlike the typically slim Hollywood actors of that time, he had biceps the size of other people's heads.

However, ignoring all these facts, Arnold did a remarkable job of creating a dream for himself. He chose a destination and created excitement. He created a vision and placed himself in that vision by holding onto an image of future success that he could live into.

Can we say that he succeeded in becoming a Hollywood star?

We can easily say that he became an action-movie star with global recognition. And in 2003, at the age of 53, he became the Governor of California. We can define this as a real success story for someone who came to U.S. at age 21 with only a suitcase and with so many disadvantages.

Now, let's take a look at the areas in which Arnold developed himself on the way to becoming a movie star.

It would be right to say that he needed to improve his speech, posture, popularity and presence in order to be a movie star.

And can we say that he needed the same set of skills to be a Governor?

Very likely, right? We can easily say that he used the same qualities in politics that he developed to be a movie star.

We can never guess what opportunities life will present us in the future. Like Arnold, we need to understand that what is more important than our goals are the things we learn during the process of pursuing our goals.

I would like to repeat the question I asked before. Is sustainable success all about results? Or is it about the things that we do passionately in the process?

Right now, take a pen and write down or even draw where you see yourself ten years from now. By drawing, you are helping your brain to categorize your goal. By visualizing and repeating your goal, you put your subconscious to work finding ways to achieve it.

Then divide your ten-year goal into shorter-term goals of around three years each. Now ask yourself, what can you learn from your current job or from your current relationships that would prepare you to achieve your first three-year goal?

Note that what you learn in this regard will contribute to your ten-year goal and to the opportunities that you will come across in your life. A Chinese proverb says, "Life gives you three opportunities to be successful. If you use them right, you get three more, but if you waste them you get no more." So the main question is, will you be ready or not when the opportunity comes along?

What should you do differently to acquire new habits that will help you to achieve your three- and ten-year goals?

One of the biggest obstacles standing between us and our objectives is our habits. We will not be able to go any farther towards our goals as long as we are unwilling to change our habits.

Write down which habits you should change and which ones you should acquire to achieve your goals. Start by focusing on a maximum of three. These will be your very-short-term goals. Try to make observations and try to take on new responsibilities to obtain these competencies in the near future.

For example, someone who intends to start his own business in ten years, with a short-term goal of being a sales manager in three years, should focus on developing his habits of appealing to emotions, talking effectively and developing his sales and leadership competencies by taking on new responsibilities.

You will notice that the path to your goals will become clearer as you change your habits, and your long-term goals will seem more reachable as you start to achieve short-term successes.

To Increase Your Self-Confidence and Motivation:

Do:
✓ Face your fears over and over again;
✓ Have a life purpose and make a plan that divides your goals into smaller pieces;
✓ Rather than the results, focus on what you should do differently in the process.

Don't Do:
✓ Don't think that you can never change your habits;
✓ Don't assess situations and your goals as being bigger than they are;
✓ Don't intend to find your motivation in money, titles or other people's interests.

8

The Impact of Our Fears on Our Behaviors

Think of a horror movie that you have seen. When was the scariest moment in the movie? Was it when you saw the beast or the killer? Or was it long before that, when you had to face your own fears?

Consider your anxiety and fear about returning to work after a long vacation. Would you agree that your first day back will most likely be much better than your fears led you to believe?

Consider the projects that you have always dreamed of doing but somehow did not dare to begin. Are you afraid of the consequences if the project goes bad? Or are you more afraid that your inner voice will prove correct, the voice that's been whispering "You will fail" ever since childhood?

The things we encounter in life mostly appear scary and impossible to us because our worries and fears envision those situations at their worst.

For example, research studies show that the most frightening thing for most people is speaking in public. Some people claim that they find it even more frightening than the prospect of death.

There are many social-phobic people who have suffered from situations such as being humiliated or unloved, or because the "responsible" part of their brain was working more than usual. At first glance we might consider them timid and cold, but when they are in a familiar environment these people can be really very warm, talented and sensitive.

Did you ever think about where our fears come from?

The most fundamental reason is the need for protection.

Consider the first people who ever lived. While they were out hunting, they encountered wild animals and got injured. So they learned by experience what they needed to be afraid of and protected from.

Now, let's look at our own environment. Whatever we do, we face almost everything with anxiety and doubt. We feel fear even by just talking about some topics.

Did we, like the first humans, *experience* the things that we are afraid of? If not, why are we so sure that we are going to fail?

At these moments, our parents' words first come to our mind. "Don't go near that dog—he bites...Don't touch the cat—she scratches...Don't get into that business you don't know...Get a day job with a salary... "A generation that grows up with the fear of getting injured and the fear of trying new things inevitably consists of individuals who are constantly afraid of failing and being disappointed.

Let's look around. Everyone wants to win, but nobody wants to lose.

Is that possible?

In reality, losing is the only true way to start winning. Have you ever heard of a boxer who became a champion without being defeated and getting knocked down? Even Mike Tyson had four defeats before his professional career. You can never win if you are afraid to lose and have no idea what it's like to lose.

Even worse, our fears grow exponentially in the form of action-and-reaction, much like in a communication context. The person who acquiesces to failure from the beginning never tries and never fails. He cannot develop himself and his self-confidence. He stays behind when others make progress.

On the other hand, leaders and artists never escape their fears. To the contrary, they seek fear like an adrenaline addict. They constantly flog themselves to innovate and to experience and achieve what's never been done before. They feel alive and feel proud of their work as they dance with the fear and push themselves to the edge.

As Seth Godin said, "The fear doesn't care: either you spend time avoiding it or embracing it." It's more important for you to decide how to make use of it. (Seth Godin, Fear the fear, feel the fear, 2013)

Our heart and brain contradict each other constantly. One says, "Start your own business..." The other says, "Stay where you are; why would you take the risk?" For the person who avoids taking action, eventually this internal conflict turns to anger and triggers passive-aggressive behaviors.

Do you ever do things like not responding to e-mails, agreeing to do something but not doing it, talking behind someone's back or seeing someone but not greeting them? Such passive-aggressive behaviors are the reflections of our anger passing through the filters of our conscious mind.

We also feel the same contradiction in planning our long-term goals, when changing jobs or making an important life decision.

When asked about our dreams, most of us say that we want success, wealth or respect. In fact, if we dig down a bit, we can all realize that most of these dreams are not ours but our parents' or society's dreams and expectations. In reality these responses only reflect our fears of being unsuccessful, ordinary or poor.

You remember that my mom ate her heart out when I told her about starting my own business. She still asks from time to time how my business is going. But I can't say whether she wants to hear positive things or negative things about it; I know she would like to see me consider a job with a guaranteed salary at the end of each month.

How Can We Overcome Fear?

Ultimately, overcoming our fears is related to how we assess the situations in our minds.

Turn Down the Volume of Your "Expectant Parent Voice": This parental voice inside our head consumes us from the inside out[40]. To improve our self-confidence, we need to learn how to fight against that voice. It's crucial to remind ourselves that failure is not the end of life, but rather it's an opportunity to gain experience in getting one step closer to winning.

---

[40] Dr. Alp Karaosmanoğlu, Psikonet Psychotherapy and Education Center

This voice causes us to believe that we are inadequate by constantly whispering to us that we most likely will fail, and this becomes very hurtful throughout our entire life.

When we start hearing this voice in our mind, we should remind ourselves of what we are really capable of doing. Like an investigator searching for evidence, we should scan through the successes we have had in our life or throughout our career. We should also think of other people who succeeded in similar situations and remind ourselves that our talents are not inferior to theirs at all.

Our commitment to stand against this parental voice is very important because it has been so convincing and authoritative since our childhood. Note that the most successful people in the world became who they are because, though they were defeated many times, they never quit trying.

Analyze Your Potential Gains and Losses: Often our fears cause us to shrink back from beginning or proposing a project at work, even if it has a significant chance of succeeding. If we succumb to our fears and ambivalence from the beginning, it's very possible we'll throw in the towel.

In such situations the right thing to do would be to make an analysis of potential gains and losses. Writing it down will again be very useful in helping to plant your action plan and goals in your subconscious.

For example, the long-term benefit of proposing your project could be the experience, entrepreneurship and the excitement of doing your own project if it's accepted. And if it isn't accepted, you might at least learn the reasons why it was rejected.

The long-term losses from not proposing your project? Missing the chance to rise in your work or to open your own business; being deprived of all the experience and the learning process; not pushing your limits and blaming yourself for not trying.

From this perspective, it's much easier to compare the benefits of proposing your project versus the losses from not proposing it. To increase your confidence, it would be useful to think about situations or projects where you've tried and succeeded before. Benefit from these experiences.

Here are a few questions to ask yourself about your past successes:

Did you know that you would succeed before you started?

Did your project conclude the way you first planned it?

What were the things that you were afraid of at the beginning of the project? Being disgraced? Being disappointed? Your inner "expectant parent voice"? (Note that none of these are more important than the opportunities that you will miss by not trying it.)

How did you suppress your fears and decide to continue? (Maybe you had no other choice, but the fact Is that you did it once and you can do it again.)

When was the most difficult time during the project? Did you ever consider giving up? Looking back now, do you say it was worth doing it despite all the difficulties?

Start Small: To increase our motivation and confidence, we should divide our goals into smaller, more realistic goals that can be achieved more easily and that will not intimidate us. Once we take some initial steps and realize that we can succeed, our self-confidence increases, and this trend motivates us even more to struggle and achieve the rest of our goals. If we set unrealistic goals and fail from the start, our motivation will also decrease rapidly. Focusing on the process, which consists of meeting smaller goals, is vitally important to achieving our goals and increasing our confidence.

Bingo is a terrific game that reflects our motivation process on our way to our goals. When we finish each row, our motivation increases as we see that we are one step closer to winning the game. While finishing a row doesn't guarantee our win, it reminds us that we are getting closer to winning, in much the same way that achieving our short-term goals does.

Have you ever heard of Kaizen?

It comes from the Japanese words *kai*, which means "change", and *zen*, which means "good". Setting big and ambitious targets may breed fear and worry. It causes us never to begin trying, or to give up quickly because of the overload.[41] On the other hand, the Kaizen Technique suggests starting small and delivering small improvements. This enables you to make continual improvement and helps you to exceed expectations.

The five-minute rule is a very practical way to apply the Kaizen Technique. Doing something for only five minutes is usually easy and does not breed fear or concern.[42] For example, think of yourself writing, studying or reading for five minutes. Although

---

[41] "Audit in psychotherapy: the concept of Kaizen"; M. M. Feldman; Psychiatric Bulletin; Royal College of Psychiatrists (1992)

[42] *One Small Step Can Change Your Life: The Kaizen Way*, Robert Maurer (2004)

you intend to do this activity for a short period of time, sometimes you may find yourself still at it even after hours have passed. On the other hand, starting these activities with the intention of doing them for hours would probably create anxiety and reluctance.

When you sit in front of your laptop to start writing a book or an article, you may find yourself tangled in social media because fear has blocked your creativity. But if you start with small actions such as identifying the topics or creating an outline, these small beginnings will reduce stress and help you to focus on your goal.

Now your brain does not feel jeopardized, and as soon as the alarm bells cease, the conscious activity channels in your brain will expand so that your innovative mind is able to start operating again.

Our brain shows two basic behaviors in the face of danger: either fight or run.

When we feel fear, we get excited and adrenaline starts to flow. This adrenaline and excitement are physically very useful whether we fight or run, but they also block the conscious activity channels that enable us to respond in ways that are acceptable in modern life. When we are anxious and fearful, we are no longer able to consciously act with creativity, innovation or logic at the moment they are most needed.

In such cases, we need to remind ourselves that the excitement that we feel and the pounding of our heart is just a reaction of our body to actually *help us* get through the situation. We must see our body's reactions as an ally and try to benefit from them in reflecting our positive energy. If we act with the understanding of what our body wants to achieve by exciting us and that this reaction is well-intentioned, then it's much easier to control our behaviors under stress.

We also have to tell ourselves that the thing we are afraid of is not vital and that life will continue even if we fail. But in practice this is easier said than done. We need to educate our brain to believe that the fearsome thing is insignificant.

Here is one way to see the difference starting small makes in helping us to overcome our fears:

Big goal (perceived as unachievable) ⇢ scares you ⇢ creative and conscious activity channels close ⇢ causes failure

Smaller goals (perceived as achievable and attainable) ⇢ easier to start and to overcome fear ⇢ conscious activity channels are available to use ⇢ brings success

What I want to emphasize here is not to keep your life goals small, but to divide your big goals into smaller ones so you can gradually change your habits and unseal the conscious activity channels in your brain. Kaizen allows us to overcome our fears by starting small.

Share Your Goals: Sharing our goals with as many people as possible will push us to realize them. In order to make us appear consistent, our mind will challenge us to keep struggling instead of giving up easily.

Looking at other people's completed projects, talking to experienced people and taking suggestions from decision makers will not only help us prepare, but will also create a consistency motive that will convince us to continue with our project.

Remember, once we make a choice or stand up for an idea, the desire for consistency influences us to stick with it. Recall the example of others who strove hard to stay consistent with their initial choices because consistency evokes mental strength.

To Overcome Fear:

Do:
- ✓ Face your fears and try; you don't have to succeed, just try;
- ✓ Plan small beginnings for your bigger goals;
- ✓ Tell your goals and commitments to as many people as you can.

Don't Do:
- ✓ Don't consider your fears bigger than they really are;
- ✓ Don't listen to the "expectant parent voice" in your mind;
- ✓ Don't quit facing your fears and thereby miss your opportunity to learn.

Our Automatic Behaviors

Have you ever heard of the *Glass Ceiling Syndrome*?

It's a concept that came out of the United States in the 1970s and originally emerged from an experiment conducted on fleas.

You may know that fleas can jump almost 200 times their height, up to 30 or 40 centimeters.

In the experiment, they placed some fleas in a ten-centimeter-high bowl covered with a glass ceiling. When the researchers heated the bottom of the bowl, the fleas started to jump. However, they could only jump ten centimeters because of the glass ceiling, which the fleas could not see.

The researchers repeated the experiment with the same fleas, but this time without the glass ceiling. The fleas continued to jump up to ten centimeters, expecting that they would again hit something even though there was no ceiling this time.

This "learned helplessness" of the fleas stemmed from their newly formed belief that they could not jump any higher than the height of the bowl.

Like the fleas in the bowl, we act according to our own experiences and according to situations that we have previously encountered. If we have categorized a situation in a certain way, in similar situations our brain immediately repeats our prior behavior.[43]

---

[43] *Influence: The Psychology of Persuasion*, Robert Cialdini, 1984

For example, if we have not been able to fix a problem after many attempts and finally categorized it as impossible, we tend to apply the same label when similar situations occur. We will also suggest that others behave the same way we did. In reality, the fact that we couldn't solve the problem doesn't indicate that the problem is unsolvable or impossible.

Similarly, we assume that an expensive product is high in quality and a cheap product is of poor quality regardless of the actual quality of the product. Our mind applies the already-accepted "expensive is better" principle to our behaviors.

For example, most people choose a wine based on its price. By falling back on automatic behaviors, a person may easily be convinced that the price of the wine is an indication of its quality.

As with the "expensive is better" principle, our automatic behaviors are the products of our subconscious mind, which aims to save us time and energy. But the conditions of the situations that we have experienced or heard before may have changed.

The most expensive wine may not always be the best quality wine on the menu. A restaurant owner who predicts that his customers will act in accord with the "expensive is better" guideline might overprice the wine to create a perception of quality.

Let's look at some famous predictions that turned out differently:

In 1981, Microsoft CEO Bill Gates said, "640k ought to be enough for anybody." Today, even gigabytes are not sufficient for us.

In 1899, U.S. Patent Office Commissioner Charles H. Duell said, "Everything that can be invented has been invented." This was the year when Henry Ford opened his first automobile factory.

In 1927, H.M Warner, owner of the famous Warner Brothers production company, said, "Who the hell wants to hear actors talk?" He thought there was no future for movies with sound.

Now let's ask ourselves this question. If the predictions of insightful and experienced industry experts can fail, how healthy is it for us non-experts to conclude that our situation is impossible?

Edison made over 3,000 attempts to invent the light bulb. Stallone's attempts to sell the script for his film *"Rocky"* were rejected around 1,500 times. What if Edison had tried 2,500 times and Stallone 1,400 times, and then concluded that the situation was hopeless and impossible? We wouldn't know them at all, or in any case we would know them differently.

We have a natural tendency to think negatively in never-tried-before situations. We should get used to thinking positively about how we can achieve things, instead of how we cannot do them. We need to strip our mind of our and others' glass ceilings, fears and anxieties. Only in this way can we make our subconscious mind an ally that constantly pushes us to achieve our goals.

Conclusion

"Once you learn how to swim, who cares how deep the water is?"
(Seth Godin, How deep is the water, 2013)

Whether you use the awareness you have gotten from this book in sales, in developing individual relationships, in getting a date or in your marriage, always keep in mind that change starts from the heart, by accepting yourself for who you really are. Only in this way can you expand your self-awareness by asking many questions and working through your subconscious mind, which has the real power over your behaviors.

Once you have sufficient awareness of yourself and your influences, you will find the ambition and desire to swim on your own, no matter how deep the water is or how much risk is involved. Who knows, maybe the waters in which you used to swim will seem shallow then.

To a happy and healthy life...

About the Author

After receiving his B.A. in Economics from Yildiz Technical University in Istanbul, Burc Uygurmen (pronounced Burch Ooy-gur-man) studied Project Management at UC Berkeley XT. He later spent ten years in professional sales and marketing roles in both the U.S. and Turkey.

Combining his education and professional experiences, in 2012 Uygurmen founded Praktika, a training firm that offers personalized corporate training sessions in the concept of Appealing to Emotions and Buying Behaviors.

In 2013, he started working with Professor Tom Stein, who is the U.S. manager of IIMP® (International Institute for Marketing Professionals), on the subject of Personal Branding. Uygurmen is also a co-author of Stein's upcoming book about Emotional Branding in the Entertainment Business.

Acknowledgments

My deep appreciation goes to the authors whose articles and books contributed a great deal to my understanding of the subject of this book. Also, many thanks to my family who provided me with the environment and the opportunity to be able write my own book.

My profound thanks to Professor Tom Stein for encouraging me to start writing my own articles and for allowing me to contribute to his book; and to my editor, Kenneth Stewart, who shared his vision and worked as my partner to produce the English language edition of this book.

Finally, a note of special thanks to everyone I met in my life that gave me a hard time and let me grow.

Resources

Chapter 1. How Does Our Brain Work?

"The Neurobiology of Trust; Paul J. Zak; SCIENTIFIC AMERICAN, INC.; 2008

"Oxytocin shapes the neural circuitry of trust and trust adaptation in humans"; Baumgartner T, Heinrichs M, Vonlanthen A, Fischbacher U, Fehr E; Neuron; 2008

"Oxytocin during the initial stages of romantic attachment: Relations to couples' interactive reciprocity"; Schneiderman I, Zagoory-Sharon O, Leckman JF, Feldmana R, Psychoneuroendocrinology; 2012

"Infobesity: Cognitive and Physical Impacts of Information Overconsumption"; Mark J. Pearrow; Massachusetts Institute of Technology

"Category-specific organization in the human brain does not require visual experience", Mahon, B. Z., Anzellotti, S., Schwarzbach, J., Zampini, M., & Caramazza, A.. Cognitive Neuropsychology Laboratory, Harvard University, 2009

Magic Words That Increase Sales, Mark Hayes 2013
http://www.shopify.com/blog/7131764-4-magic-words-that-increase-sales

Thinking Fast and Slow, Daniel Khaneman, 2011

Brain Tricks—This Is How Your Brain Works, Mitchell Moffit and Gregory Brown

Chapter 2. Appealing to Emotions

The Art of Thinking Clearly, Rolf Dobelli, 2011

urbanlegends.about.com/od/music/a/violinist_metro.htm

Dr.Nusret Kaya, Evrensel Eşit Kuyruklu Canlı 2, 2011

How are habits formed: Modelling habit formation in the real world, *Phillippa Lally (2009)*

The Top Five Regrets of the Dying, Bronnie Ware, 2012

Chapter 3. What's Behind Our Behaviors?

"The Nobel Prize in Physiology or Medicine 1904". Nobelprize.org. Nobel Media AB 2013. Web. 19 Nov 2013.
<http://www.nobelprize.org/nobel_prizes/medicine/laureates/1904/>

Westen, Drew (1999). "The Scientific Status of Unconscious Processes: Is Freud Really Dead?" Journal of the American Psychoanalytic Association 47 (4)

Modell, Arnold H. "Psychoanalysis, Neuroscience and the Unconscious Self." Psychoanalytic review 99.4 (2012): 475-83.PsycINFO.

The Archetypes and the Collective Unconscious, C. G. Jung, London 1996

Dr. Clotaire Rapaille. "Marketing to the Reptilian Brain." Forbes 03 July 2006: 44. Business Source Premier. EBSCO. Web. 15 June 2010.

Rhetoric, Aristotle, 350 B.C.

Chapter 4. Emotional Branding

Lovemarks – The Future Beyond Brands, Kevin Roberts, Saatchi & Saatchi, 2006

Influence: The Psychology of Persuasion, Consistency, Robert Cialdini, 1984

Karen Wynn & Paul Bloom
http://www.cbsnews.com/video/watch/?id=50151800n

Survey of Castellow, Wuensch and Moore, 1991 and Downs and Lyons, 1990

The Physiology of Willpower: Linking Blood Glucose to Self-Control"; Gailliot, Matthew T.; Baumeister, Roy F (2007)

The Hero and the Outlaw: Building Extraordinary Brands Through the Power of Archetypes, M. Mark and C. Pearson, 2001

Chapter 5. Controlling Our Behaviors

Primal Leadership: Realizing the Power of Emotional Intelligence. R.E Boyatzis, D. Goleman, A. McKee, Boston: Harvard Business School Press, 2002

Chapter 6. Building Empathy

Empathy in the Context of Philosophy, Lou Agosta, Palgrave/Macmillan, 2010

Luft, J.; Ingham, H. (1955). "The Johari Window, a graphic model of interpersonal awareness". Proceedings of the western training laboratory in group development (Los Angeles: UCLA).

Chapter 7. Being Passionate

www.ted.com/talks/maya_penn_meet_a_young_entrepreneur_cartoon
ist_designer_activist.html

Survey of Michigan University and Prof. Jean M. Twenge: "Generational Differences in Young Adults' Life Goals, Concern for Others, and Civic Orientation", 1966–2009

Stephen King from A to Z: An Encyclopedia of His Life and Work, George W. Beahm

Chapter 8. The Impact of Our Fears on Our Behaviors

"Audit in psychotherapy: the concept of Kaizen", M. M. Feldman, Psychiatric Bulletin, Royal College of Psychiatrists, 1992

"One Small Step Can Change Your Life: The Kaizen Way", Robert Maurer

Influence: The Psychology of Persuasion, Robert Cialdini, 1984

"Expectant Parental Voice": Dr. Alp Karaosmanoğlu, Psikonet Psychotherapy and Education Center